I CAN MANAGE LIFE

Learning to Choose and Grow

by

Dennis Hooker

from
jist

Publisher: J. Michael Farr
Project Director/Interior Design: Spring Dawn Reader
Managing Editor: Sara Hall
Editor: Lee Churchill
Cover Design: Dean Johnson Design Group
Composition: Joanetta Hendel

I Can Manage Life—Learning to Choose and Grow
©1992, **JIST Works, Inc.**, Indianapolis, IN

This book has a companion *Instructor's Guide* available separately from the publisher.

Ordering Information: An order form has been provided at the end of this book containing other related materials.

JIST Works, Inc.
720 North Park Avenue • Indianapolis, IN 46202-3431
Phone: **(317)264-3720** FAX: **(317)264-3709**

ISBN: 0-942784-77-4

A Personal Note to the Reader of This Book

I am the author of *I Can Manage Life*. This is more than just a book or a workbook. It is a series of experiences about life decisions — YOUR life decisions. There are no facts to memorize or answers that can be graded. Your work cannot be evaluated as "better" or "worse" than other students in the class. Each response is YOUR personal response.

You can (and probably will) be graded based on the amount of energy you put into the program. You could be evaluated on how you have improved in your areas of growth. You certainly will be seen by yourself, other members of the group and your leader (instructor, facilitator, etc.) by the progress in your ability to make life choices and your growth through interaction with them.

Perhaps your grammar, punctuation and proper word usage can be improved. So, grades are appropriate for evaluating *how* you write — not *what* you write. Your ideas and opinions and dreams and plans and reflections cannot be wrong. It is impossible!

I used the concepts of *Family*, *Co-workers*, *Friends*, *Mates*, and *Community* because students in my own classes really like it. I've had dozens tell me it was the first Family that they had really felt. Bonds were forged that lasted long after the program was over.

The Learning Process

I Can Manage Life is designed to be cooperative (as opposed to competitive). This encourages open communication about the options available to you in life and how to experience life to the fullest.

Experiencing life to the fullest includes learning to have more fun, enjoyment, satisfaction, love and growth. It is a PROCESS. It takes learning to make decisions and being open to growth. And it takes learning to allow me to describe the present success I feel and to stretch me to discover the depths of meaning in the words. That is LANGUAGE.

Language is the communication from me to you — you to me — and us to the world. Language is read by others with the subtle and broad movements of our bodies, the flow of air out of our lips and the scribbling we put on cave walls. It is books such as this one, *I Can Manage Life—Learning to Choose and Grow.*

Have fun with it, enjoy yourself and each other, get satisfaction from completing experiences, stretching beyond yourself to love yourself and others in a new way and to experience growth.

As the author of this program I choose to express this message:

✎ Have fun!

✎ Experience enjoyment in your senses!

✎ Get satisfaction in planning and completing tasks.

✎ Love—stretch beyond your usual self!

✎ Grow—relax, grab the feelings as they come!

How This Book Is Arranged

The main components of this book are sections titled *Challenge, Explore, Thinking About This,* and *Sharing.*

The experiences are introduced by a ***Challenge*** — a simple statement to set the mood or to tell you the author's thoughts. You will have tasks which let you research, create, discover, define, and interview. Your ***Explore*** responses should be written in this manual. Keep it short. Try and say what you want to say in the space provided, but you can use other paper if necessary. ***Thinking About This*** is your chance to reflect on the topic you have been exploring. Let your mind wander—guided by, but definitely not limited to the introspective questions presented. You will be writing your responses in a journal—a bound notebook. When ***Sharing***, you will bring your explorations and journaled thoughts to share with the suggested members:

Family: A group of four to six members assigned to you by a drawing (as it is in your real life family). You will be with this family throughout the program (as in real life).

Co-workers: Four to six members who work with you on job and career-related tasks. This group may change (you may get "fired") over time and you will need to adapt.

Friends: These are friends of your choice to share special problems or tasks. The key to this, as in all these group relationships, is to develop trust, respect and cooperation.

Mates: You will be assigned (as in the "old country") a life partner. You will have several partnering experiences such as picking a house, facing financial responsibilities, maturing problems — and maybe even have a baby who will grow into adolescence in a couple of weeks!

Community: The total group is your community with whom you will be sharing your individual and/or small group processes and products.

All of these groups will become opportunities for caring and sharing. During this interaction you will be promoting your expression (language) of decision-making skills and experiencing personal growth at all levels (academic, job/career choice, interaction with mates, family, friends and community).

You will have a journal on which to record your thoughts. Again, I remind you, your opinions and thoughts cannot be graded. I suggest you use a separate, personal notebook or diary for your very private thoughts.

At the end of each major section of this book is a "Simulation" that helps pull together all you have learned. The simulation is meant to be a real-life experience. Although we are "manufacturing" it (making it happen) it is genuine in that you will actually BE the characters involved and will really DO the tasks suggested. It is not pretend — it is simulation.

Table of Contents

SECTION III—*The World Around Us*   127

SECTION I

This Is Me

Welcome to the expedition! You are about to start off on a unique quest. You will be seeking YOU. How will you do that? Challenge material will give you thoughts to bounce around. What might look like ordinary worksheets turn out to be tasks that allow you to DISCOVER your feelings, ideas, imagination, and plans. And you are not alone. Also on this expedition will be classmates also getting a clearer sense of who they are.

As you respond to the activities before you, questions will awaken you and lead you into new vistas of understanding and choice. Each page will refresh your vision, zig-zagging you from your imagination to your thinking, from your preferences to your plans, from your interactions to your deepest wishes. Satisfaction awaits you as you proceed in a safe setting of mutual trust.

Laughter will break out at unexpected times as your groups draw closer and trust builds. I cheer you on and wish you joy on your quest. A YOU-ER YOU will be rewarded with a new sense of capability and direction. May you richly enjoy the adventure.

YOU ARE UNIQUE

Challenge. *"There is only one person in the whole wide world JUST LIKE YOU - that's you! And, I like you just the way that you are...that's right!"*
—**Mr. Rogers,** *Public Broadcasting Service*

Explore

✎ Here are some adjectives that describe some general personality traits. Circle those words that could fit you. Have fun! It is not scientific!

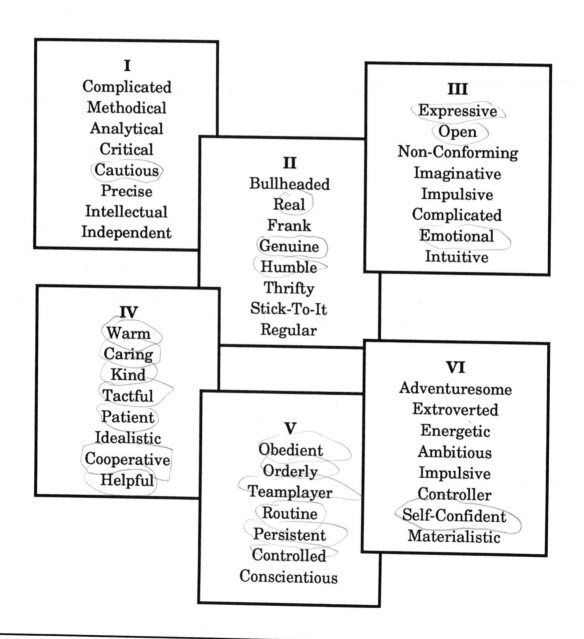

I
Complicated
Methodical
Analytical
Critical
Cautious
Precise
Intellectual
Independent

II
Bullheaded
Real
Frank
Genuine
Humble
Thrifty
Stick-To-It
Regular

III
Expressive
Open
Non-Conforming
Imaginative
Impulsive
Complicated
Emotional
Intuitive

IV
Warm
Caring
Kind
Tactful
Patient
Idealistic
Cooperative
Helpful

V
Obedient
Orderly
Teamplayer
Routine
Persistent
Controlled
Conscientious

VI
Adventuresome
Extroverted
Energetic
Ambitious
Impulsive
Controller
Self-Confident
Materialistic

✎ Which two categories (from I-VI) have the most traits circled? List 10 of the traits and research their meanings.

1._____

2._____

3._____

4._____

5._____

6._____

7._____

8._____

9._____

10._____

✎ Circle the number of the five traits that YOU like the most.

> ***Thinking About This.*** *I will think of times in my life when I used each of the five traits. Was it to my advantage and that of another person(s)? How did it feel? What was my purpose? Where was I? How can these traits be considered in my choice of friends? Choice of classes/training? Career? Pastimes?*
>
> ***Sharing (Family).*** *Share five of your best traits (not necessarily those you like the most) and give examples when you used each. Look at the list again to decide three traits that you definitely do NOT want to have. Tell why.*

✎ Count the number of traits that you circled in each section. Use the following Key to Traits to compare the sections with your highest and lowest traits circled.

1._____

2._____

3._____

4._____

5._____

Key to Traits: I = Problem-Solver; **II** = Practical; **III** = Creative; **IV** = Helper; **V** = Enterpriser, and **VI** = Organizer. (These are for interest areas only, not meant for scientific study.)

IS IT POSSIBLE?

> **Challenge.** *One person looks at a lump of clay and sees a hunk of dirt. Another looks at the clay and sees a beautiful vase waiting to be made.*

Explore

✎ Think of something in your life that didn't go right for you. Describe how you wanted it to go.

_____

_____

_____

_____

✎ *"If you are not part of the solution you are part of the problem."* Think of two problems in your life that would straighten out IF you allowed them. (That is, if you didn't interfere with the solution.) Describe ways each of these situations could go better.

1. _____

_____

_____

_____

2. _____

_____

_____

_____

> **Thinking About This.** *Which friend of mine only sees the hunk of dirt? I will share some ideas on how to assist my friend to see other possibilities.*
>
> **Sharing (Family).** *A boy was digging in a stall piled to the ceiling with manure. He said, "With all this manure there must be a pony here somewhere." He is an optimist! What is that? What is a pessimist?" A pep-tomist? Share examples when you were each of these.*

THAT'S MY OPINION

Challenge: *Is there such a thing as a "wrong" opinion?*

Explore

✎ Here are some people's opinions. Think about each one then place a checkmark under the Agree or Disagree column. Be prepared to defend your opinion with examples from from your own experiences.

OPINIONS	AGREE	DISAGREE
I can't have anything until I let go of it.		
Being good does not always pay.		
Some people are greater than others.		
I can't control anybody.		
I am worth full-price.		
I must take care of myself.		
When I put someone on a pedestal I am somehow diminishing myself.		
When I have love I am full.		
It is a joy to assist you in your growth.		
Men often communicate in a different style than women.		
It is more important for me to understand you than for you to understand me.		
I can escape successfully from reality.		
I can forgive myself without understanding myself.		
A good student gets good grades.		
I am in charge around here.		
All people learn in the same way.		

✎ Was it difficult to have a firm opinion? How? Why? Which ones? Rewrite five opinions that you strongly disagreed with so that you can now strongly agree with each. Be prepared to defend and illustrate your opinion.

1. _____
_____
_____
_____

2. _____
_____
_____
_____

3. _____
_____
_____
_____

4. _____
_____
_____
_____

5. _____
_____
_____
_____

✎ Circle the number of the three opinions that you feel the strongest about.

> **Thinking About This.** *Which opinions did I feel strongly about? Which one(s) gave me no feeling? Where was I wrong? Right? How can I tell?*
>
> **Sharing (Family).** *Find one other family member with some exact opposite opinions of yours. Try to change their mind! (The rest of the family will observe without saying anything.) Now, get people on your side to convince the "other" side. Did you? Why? How? Get feedback from others on your methods that worked. What didn't work? Who was right? Wrong? Why?*

TOUGH DECISIONS

> ***Challenge.*** *At times in your life you have to make some difficult decisions. Now is one of them. You are faced with eight tough, real-life dilemmas. You must do something. Be loving and gentle, but be yourself.*

Explore

✎ A reaction could be defined as a first response without thinking. An action is a response given more thought. Tell what you would do in each of the following situations. Be specific in setting up the situation and describing your reactions and your actions. (How I might react; how I could act.)

An acquaintance is showing off to you.

Reaction: _____

_____

_____

Action: _____

_____

_____

You feel your parents are disgusted with you.

Reaction: _____

_____

_____

Action: _____

_____

_____

You are very angry.

Reaction: _____

_____

_____

Action: _____

_____

_____

A pesky person wants to argue with you.

Reaction: _____

_____

_____

Action: _____

_____

_____

Your best friend is really bugging you.

Reaction: _____

_____

_____

Action: _____

_____

_____

You want your friend to know you like him/her.

Reaction: _____

_____

_____

Action: _____

_____

_____

You want someone to know you can be trusted.

Reaction: _____

_____

_____

Action: _____

_____

_____

You want a discouraged person to laugh.

Reaction: _____

_____

_____

Action: _____

_____

_____

An acquaintance with a substance abuse problem becomes rude.

Reaction: _____

_____

_____

Action: _____

_____

_____

You fall in love with a very fine person.

Reaction: _____

_____

_____

Action: _____

_____

_____

Thinking About This. *What other tough decisions do I have to make? How do I handle each of them? What are other differences between reactions and actions? Which is better? When?*

Sharing (Friends). *Share your reactions and actions with your friends. Applaud each answer equally as a show of respect for each person's way of handling tough decisions. Pick two of the above situations to role play among Friends—then with the Community.*

OBSERVATION

> **Challenge.** *You see, hear and touch millions of things each day. You don't have to think about most of these observations. They occur naturally and without thought.*

Explore

✎ The teacher/leader will show you pictures of five people's faces. Write down as many things about each person that you are aware of. Include your observations and impressions.

Person 1

_____

_____

_____

Person 2

_____

_____

_____

Person 3

_____

_____

_____

Person 4

_____

_____

_____

Person 5

_____

_____

_____

✎ View five pictures of people doing things together. Describe what is being done, what probably happened before and what will probably happen afterward.

Picture 1

What do you think is happening? _____

_____

_____

What do you think happened before? _____

_____

_____

What do you think will happen next? _____

_____

_____

Picture 2

What do you think is happening? _____

_____

_____

What do you think happened before? _____

_____

_____

What do you think will happen next? _____

_____

_____

Picture 3

What do you think is happening? _____

_____

_____

What do you think happened before? _____

_____

_____

What do you think will happen next? _____

_____

_____

Picture 4

What do you think is happening? _____

_____

_____

What do you think happened before? _____

_____

_____

What do you think will happen next? _____

_____

_____

Picture 5

What do you think is happening? _____

_____

_____

What do you think happened before? _____

_____

_____

What do you think will happen next? _____

_____

_____

Thinking About This. *Was I quick to assign qualities to the five people (or did I assign liabilities)? What doubts do I have about my interpretation of the situations in the five action pictures? What is a reaction? Action? What is the difference? Which is better in dealing with individuals? With situations? Do I judge too quickly? Slowly? Harshly? Leniently? Do I care how I am seen? How? When? Why? Do I care how I see? How? When? Why?*

Sharing (Family). *Discuss these terms: Judgment, Prejudgment, Prejudice, Bias, Love, Fear, Reactions and Actions, Stereotypes, Rejection, and Acceptance.*

LOOK AT ME

> ***Challenge.*** *We are sometimes aware of others around us - even talk and interact with them. But, do we really see them? It takes directed attention to tune into them as unique individuals.*

Explore

✎ The leader will show you a large busy photo from a magazine. You will only have a 10 second look. Then list everything that you can recall in the picture.

_____

_____

_____

_____

_____

_____

_____

_____

_____

_____

✎ Look around the room for 10 seconds, and then list as many things on the wall as you can.

_____

_____

_____

_____

_____

_____

_____

_____

_____

✎ A volunteer will leave the room. List every detail of the missing person's appearance that you can remember.

_____

_____

_____

_____

_____

✎ Describe here how you perceive yourself. (Be gentle and admiring.)

_____

_____

_____

_____

_____

✎ Describe how your parents perceive you. (Use a specific time or situation.)

_____

_____

_____

_____

_____

✎ How has your perception of yourself changed over the years?

_____

_____

_____

_____

As a son or daughter

_____

_____

_____

_____

_____

As a sister or brother

_____
_____
_____
_____
_____

As a student

_____
_____
_____
_____
_____

As a friend

_____
_____
_____
_____
_____

Thinking About This. *How do I look at others? What do I see? What can I see better? What do I look for that is honest and good? What do they see in me? What is my general perception of myself?*

Sharing (Family). *Discuss these topics from LOOK AT ME. What do you really want to see in others? Give others honest, gentle feedback about self-improvement in specific areas of their lives. Thank them. What is the best way to do that?*

WHAT DO THEY MEAN?

> **Challenge.** *If we can just allow ourselves to be ourselves we can really be useful in this world.* — **Mr. Rogers**, *Public Broadcasting Service*

Explore

✎ Give a title to Mr. Roger's statement:

_____

_____

✎ What does he mean? (Rewrite it in your own words below.)

_____

_____

_____

_____

_____

_____

"The true function of a person's education should be the process of helping him/her to discover his/her uniqueness, aiding him/her toward its development, and teaching him/her how to share it with others." — **Leo Buscaglia**, *LOVE*

✎ What are two of the author's main points?

1. _____

_____

2. _____

_____

✎ Now say it in your own words:

_____

_____

_____

_____

_____

_____

✎ What would you title Mr. Buscaglia's statement? Why?

_____

_____

_____

_____

_____

_____

> ***Thinking About This.*** *What do I think about the subject "Learning to be the most I can be?" How does this agree or disagree with Mr. Rogers and Mr. Buscaglia?*
>
> ***Sharing (Family).*** *Share your own statements about being yourself. How does it feel to have your statement being compared with the experts quoted above? How can education help a person to be themselves? How can we discover and develop our own uniqueness? How can we share it with others? Think of a good education system that would allow each person's needs to be met. Design the perfect classroom that uses Buscaglia's, Roger's and your ideas.*

I CAN SEE ME

Challenge. *"If you could look infinitely far forward, if you could look infinitely far out in space, there's no question what you would see: you would see the back of your head."* — **Paul Williams**, *Das Energie*

Explore

✎ You have just been given the rare gift of seeing yourself as an intelligent, sensitive space traveler would see you. What qualities does the traveler observe in you?

As a friend

_____

_____

_____

As a co-worker

_____

_____

_____

As a family member

_____

_____

_____

As a creator

_____

_____

_____

As a learner

_____

_____

_____

 © 1992, JIST Works, Inc. • Indianapolis, Indiana

As a planner

_____

_____

_____

As a doer

_____

_____

_____

As a traveler on Spaceship Earth

_____

_____

_____

Thinking About This. Am I ALREADY an OK person? Why? How? How can I be worthwhile just because I exist? How can accepting my self-worth affect my life? I now take a deep breath and, for a brief moment, accept my value as a perfect creation. I will take more of these quick time-outs to feel good about myself. Can this help me to improve my ability to serve others? Is that good? Why? How?

Sharing (Family). Share your personal thoughts expressed above. Who caught the instant of acceptance? What feelings came with that moment of peace? What thoughts? Who felt distracted with lots of thoughts instead of quietness? Be encouraged — experts tell us that in quiet we discover the thoughts that are always there clamoring for attention. In fact, this awareness of internal noise is the first step in entering inner quietness — the creative mood. Discuss this concept. Research these terms: Biofeedback, Alpha and Delta Waves, Endorphins, Relaxation, Response and Self-hypnosis.

RELAXING CREATIVELY

> ***Challenge.*** *A relaxed human being is a valuable receiving "mechanism." Relax and tune into all the things that are going on—all the awarenesses that are coming into your mind and body...feelings, pain, aches, sounds, thoughts, strengths, etc.*

Explore

✎ List 10 awarenesses that you tuned into.

1._____
2._____
3._____
4._____
5._____
6._____
7._____
8._____
9._____
10._____

✎ List 10 things you are thinking RIGHT NOW! Jot them down as they pop into your mind—no matter how wild they are.

1._____
2._____
3._____
4._____
5._____
6._____
7._____
8._____
9._____
10._____

 © 1992, JIST Works, Inc. • Indianapolis, Indiana

✎ What percentage of the time do you spend thinking of the following?

Past: _____% Present: _____% Future: _____% = Total 100%

✎ Pick one of the awarenesses you wrote in the first list. Write it below.

Awareness: _____

✎ Now write 10 brief thoughts about this awareness.

1._____   6. _____
2._____   7. _____
3._____   8. _____
4._____   9. _____
5._____   10. _____

✎ Do the same task for a thought from the second list. Write it below.

Awareness: _____

✎ Now write 10 brief thoughts about this awareness.

1._____   6. _____
2._____   7. _____
3._____   8. _____
4._____   9. _____
5._____   10. _____

Thinking About This. *What is the nicest to think about? What feelings do I get with nice thoughts? When do I get most of them? Where am I? Doing what? How often? How can I do it more often? (Be specific.) Here is my definite plan on how and when to relax more frequently.*

Sharing (Family). *Share your awarenesses. Discuss your similarities. Differences. What are the feelings each member gets when relaxed? Contrast this to the feelings when tense. Discuss specific plans to get good relaxation time.*

THE MEANING OF SUCCESS

> ***Challenge.*** *One indication of your success is that you are NOW expressing what you already know. And Success is the confidence that you know what you know!*

Explore

✎ Listed below are five words that describe the ways you can communicate. Your task is to define each word in its simplest form. Think of a time when you communicated in that particular way. Write about that example.

1. Expressive: _____

_____

Example: _____

_____

2. Unique: _____

_____

Example: _____

_____

3. Fluent: _____

_____

Example: _____

_____

4. Proficient: _____

_____

Example: _____

_____

5. Decisive: _____

_____

Example: _____

_____

✎ List five more words that describe successful language usage. Give workable definitions and share examples of the words.

1. _____: _____

_____

Example: _____

_____

2. _____: _____

_____

Example: _____

_____

3. _____: _____

_____

Example: _____

_____

4. _____: _____

_____

Example: _____

_____

5. _____: _____

_____

Example: _____

_____

Thinking About This. *I will list synonyms for each of these words. How can expressing myself even better make me even more successful? What areas of my life can benefit when I express myself more clearly? What do I need to do? What is my plan for self-improvement?*

Sharing (Family). *Share your plans for self-improvement. Discuss the self-searching questions in Thinking About This. Share your new words and your thoughts with the Community.*

EXPERT FEES

> **Challenge.** *A huge diesel engine would not start. Experts were imported from around the country. No one could start it. A little old man with wire-rimmed spectacles approached the fancy engineers. "I can start it and my fee is $1,000." They laughed, but bid him try. He walked over to the engine, kicked a valve and the engine roared into life. "How can you charge $1,000 for kicking an engine?" they cried. He answered with a satisfied smile, "Oh it's only $1 for kicking the engine. I charge $999 for knowing WHERE to kick it."*

Explore

✎ What are YOU the best at? (Describe fully below.)

_____

_____

_____

_____

_____

✎ How can you do this more often for more people?

_____

_____

_____

_____

_____

✎ What will you expect in return?

_____

_____

_____

_____

_____

✎ Describe your lifestyle as you do this work (i.e., interaction with others, travel, home, partners, co-workers, etc.).

_____

_____

_____

_____

_____

_____

✎ Consider a completely different lifestle doing this same work. Describe it here.

_____

_____

_____

_____

_____

_____

Thinking About This. *What do I need to KNOW or DO to get better at this? Where? How? When? How could I begin to be financially rewarded NOW for my expertise in this area?*

Sharing (Co-workers). *Share what you are good at. Go into detail. What are your plans to do it for other people? What do you expect in return? (Is it more than money?) Discuss the pros and cons of working for financial gain and for personal satisfaction. What is a workaholic? Discuss their feelings... motivations... cures. How are our lives being centered around areas of expertise? How much time should we invest in it?*

GET SPECIFIC

> **Challenge.** *Earl Nightingale, an expert on success, said that a person studying for ONE hour a day on a SPECIFIC topic will, within five years, be a world recognized authority on that specific subject.*

Explore

✎ Decide one general topic about which you would like to be very knowledgeable.

The general subject: _____

✎ Now, get more specific. Which facet of that subject would interest you the most?

More specifically: _____

_____

✎ The specific aspect you picked can be further divided into at least three divisions. List what they are.

1. _____
2. _____
3. _____

Pick one of these to concentrate on: _____

✎ Research the components of that specific division. How can it be divided FURTHER into areas of study?

1. _____
2. _____
3. _____

✎ Put a star by one or two of these further divided areas that interest you the most.

> **Thinking About This.** *What is my plan to become an expert on my chosen subject? (Be very specific.) How many major steps would it take? What kinds of resources would I use? Whose help would I need? What decisions and responsibilities are mine? Others?*
>
> **Sharing (Family).** *Share your topics and plans to become experts with the Community.*

© 1992, JIST Works, Inc. • Indianapolis, Indiana

TEST ME

> ***Challenge.*** *Test results can be helpful to you. In the lower grades test results help teachers place you in the most suitable classes. Some test results also helped measure your progress in the subject areas. But, now you have the abilty to make your own decisions. Test results can help you make your own choices for classes or training courses.*

Explore

✎ List the results of three tests you have taken in the last couple of years. Meet with the proper school officials to get your test results. Get at least one academic, one aptitude and one interest test. (Take the tests if you haven't already.)

Academic

_____

_____

_____

_____

Aptitude

_____

_____

_____

_____

Interest

_____

_____

_____

_____

> ***Thinking About This.*** *What do test results reveal about ourselves? How do test results influence our decision-making ability?Are they a good measure of success? Why? Answer the following questions about each type of test.*

✎ Academic Test(s)

What I learned about myself.

_____

_____

_____

How this information helps my schooling/training decisions.

_____

_____

_____

✎ Aptitude Test(s)

What I learned about myself.

_____

_____

_____

How this information helps my schooling/training decisions.

_____

_____

_____

✎ Interest Test(s)

What I learned about myself.

_____

_____

_____

How this information helps my schooling/training decisions.

_____

_____

_____

> ***Sharing (Family).*** *Share with your family any information from your tests that suprised you. What are your strengths and weaknesses? Which strengths and weaknesses did you already know about? Share what the overall picture from the tests seem to reveal. Discuss options for academic growth using your interests.*

GOOD CHOICES

> **Challenge.** *The best choices are made when you have the most information to assist you in making the decisions. You may have discovered many new areas to explore in choosing your life options. Perhaps you need to know more about these things.*

Explore

✎ List those things of interest that require more research. What do you need to know? Where can you get that information?

ACADEMIC CLASSES	WHAT MORE I NEED TO FIND OUT	WHERE I CAN GET THE INFORMATION

✎ Under the headings below, list the things you need to consider when planning your future.

Vocational Training

_____

_____

_____

_____

Schools

_____

_____

_____

_____

Friends

_____

_____

_____

_____

My Experience

_____

_____

_____

_____

Thinking About This. Which information am I most eager to get? Can I be pretty sure which sources will be most valuable? Which sources do I prefer? Resist? Does my experience starting this research contribute to my self-understanding? Which of the sources are used most commonly? Least? Is there a payoff even if I don't get the sought after information? I will notice feelings as I make these inquiries.

Sharing (Family). Tell what your first impulse was when you saw the list of resources. See if group members consider resources in a different light from you. Do some people prefer personal sources? Impersonal?

IT'S MY HEAD

> **Challenge.** *I am told that everything I have ever seen or experienced is stored away in my memory. All that is needed is a method to get this information out of storage.*

Explore

✎ What is in your head? Personal brainstorm listing all the ideas that pop into your mind as fast as they come. Don't judge or leave any of them off your list. Put all on paper—no matter what your head says.

_____   _____

_____   _____

_____   _____

_____   _____

_____   _____

_____   _____

_____   _____

_____   _____

✎ What is in my head this moment about these specific subjects:

My Schooling / Training

_____   _____

_____   _____

_____   _____

_____   _____

_____   _____

_____   _____

_____   _____

_____   _____

_____   _____

My Personal / Social Life

_____   _____
_____   _____
_____   _____
_____   _____
_____   _____
_____   _____
_____   _____
_____   _____
_____   _____

My Future

_____   _____
_____   _____
_____   _____
_____   _____
_____   _____
_____   _____
_____   _____
_____   _____
_____   _____

Thinking About This. *I will allow thoughts to occur that I haven't had in years — ever since I first experienced them. I will pick a word and let words pop into my mind that connect to the previous word. Then, I will allow pictures to pop into my mind with each word. I will put these connected ramblings in my journal.*

Sharing (Family). *Share your rambling thoughts expressed in Explore. Then, tell of your connected thoughts from Thinking About This. What feeling do you have in resurrecting hidden thoughts and word pictures? Why? What is daydreaming? Can it be valuable? How? When? What is imagination? Memory? Fantasy? Flow of Consciousness?*

PLAN YOUR SCHOOLING

> ***Challenge.*** *You are asked by the school system to create your own course of studies for your education. Start from the grade you are in now and continue until you get your full training.*

Explore

✎ Your task is to decide on a possible career field, give a general course of study for each year and describe the courses you will need to arrive at your career goals. Research high school, technical school and college catalogs, the *Dictionary of Occupational Titles*, etc. Remember—you are to INVENT YOUR OWN COURSES! Let the research feed your creativity.

Your possible job/career: _____

✎ Major courses you need in order to get into that career field. (Do not depend on existing courses now available.)

COURSE NAME	COURSE DESCRIPTION	NUMBER OF SEMESTERS

✎ Share your list of courses with others who have a similar career/job choice. Add more course ideas.

COURSE NAME	COURSE DESCRIPTION	NUMBER OF SEMESTERS

Thinking About This. *I want to begin now to start working toward my future. I will make a specific plan that includes courses I can take now, a part-time job and / or hobbies and activities that get me closer to my objectives. I will be specific in where, how, why, when, and what. I will write a description of how this NEW plan compares to what I am now doing — noting where I am on and off the track.*

Sharing (Co-workers). *Compare your courses and plans. What is actually available now that is close to those courses you listed? You can help each other until each person's plans are as clearly defined as possible at this point.*

FUTURE COURSES

> **Challenge.** *Imagine that you are about to begin advanced training or schooling. Get catalogs from several schools. Use the library or send away for catalogs. Check the catalogs for courses relating to a specific life choice, career, or lifestyle.*

Explore

✎ Explore some courses that look interesting to you.

_____

_____

_____

_____

_____

✎ What I need to do or to prepare for the courses.

_____

_____

_____

_____

_____

✎ List three specific ways that my hobbies and interests can prepare me for these courses.

1. _____

_____

_____

2. _____

_____

_____

3. _____

_____

_____

✎ Further imagine that there are three major decisions you have to make to get you up to and through these courses. List each of these in Decisions I, II, and III. Then briefly discuss strategies for carrying out the decisions.

Decision I: _____

_____

_____

_____

_____

_____

Decision II: _____

_____

_____

_____

_____

_____

Decision III: _____

_____

_____

_____

_____

_____

Thinking About This. *I will list my personal strengths and weaknesses related to achieving my aspirations. Then, I will see how this personal profile fits my specific life choices, career, or lifestyle. I will work with my Family to devise charts, graphs, and grids to illustrate the connections between who I am and what the world asks of me. I will create a letter to a fictional college or technical school registrar that convinces them to give me advanced credits for my present skills, aptitudes and experiences.*

Sharing (Family). *Share your research that combines your personal profile with your specific life choices, career, or lifestyles. Give helpful feedback to each other to revise or add to your letter. You will be coming back to this later so be as complete as you can now.*

SERVICE TO THE WORLD

Challenge. Some aggresive people I know, like hogs I've seen, can jump into the hog trough of selfishness, go down too deep, stay down too long and push others away so that they may come up with more themselves.

Explore

✎ List eight ways to get money for yourself "out-of-people."

1._____   5._____
2._____   6._____
3._____   7._____
4._____   8._____

✎ Now, think in terms of what you can give of yourself that is a service to others. You are not looking for financial reward—you only wish to provide a service to the world as a part-time or full-time thing. Let the ideas just roll off your mind—without thinking or analyzing. Try to think of at least 20 things in five minutes.

1._____   11._____
2._____   12._____
3._____   13._____
4._____   14._____
5._____   15._____
6._____   16._____
7._____   17._____
8._____   18._____
9._____   19._____
10._____   20._____

Thinking About This. Why is service a better, more workable way of "looking for work" than the "getting a job to make money" way?

Sharing (Family). Discuss your listed ways to give to the world. Discuss what may be the natural reward for practicing this service-to-others approach.

A SERVICE ECONOMY

> **Challenge.** *The American economy is turning into a service economy. Factories and industries are not as important. Only certain careers/jobs are really serving others. Some say that no job exists that does not "serve."*

Explore

✎ What is an adequate definition of service? Write two opposing definitions of your own below.

Negative definition of service: _____

_____

_____

_____

_____

Positive definition of service: _____

_____

_____

_____

_____

✎ Write three careers/jobs that interest you (for any reason) in which service is an obvious element.

1. _____
2. _____
3. _____

✎ Write three careers/jobs that interest you (for any reason) in which service is not an obvious element.

1. _____
2. _____
3. _____

✎ List five things you like to do that could be useful to others (and you get rewarded in the process).

1. _____

2. _____

3. _____

4. _____

5. _____

✎ Think of three people who really like their jobs. Find out (or imagine) how they could have gotten into that area of work at your age (entry level).

THE PERSON	HOW THEY STARTED
1. _____	_____
	_____
	_____
2. _____	_____
	_____
	_____
3. _____	_____
	_____
	_____

Thinking About This. *Have I already done volunteer work or paid work in which service is obvious? What was it? Am I aware at times of being "served" by someone I don't know to feed, clothe and house me? How do I feel about serving others? Would it matter to me if the service were "hidden" or very "obvious?" What kinds of satisfaction come from "service?"*

Sharing (Co-workers). *Team up with two other co-workers and make a plan to interview a few workers about "service." Together draw up appropriate questions to discover who and what they serve. Report back to the group how that particular job serves other levels in the economy. Discover how much the interviewees have considered in their roles as servers. Report if and how your conception of service has changed as a result of the interviews.*

NINE LIVES

> **Challenge.** *Cats may not have nine lives, but most people have several different careers in a lifetime (or phases of the same career). For example, a young man helped in a detention home. He worked with the Juvenile Court and went to a junior college at night. He graduated from college to work as a teacher, counselor and then a psychologist. Later, he taught counseling, psychology and specialized in helping youth learn about life options. He later wrote books assisting young adults to learn more about themselves so that they could express themselves more effectively and make better life choices.*

Explore

✎ Choose a career of interest to you. Write a beginning "job" (one you could start at today). Then, fantasize a possible series of jobs that go naturally from one rung of the ladder to the next.

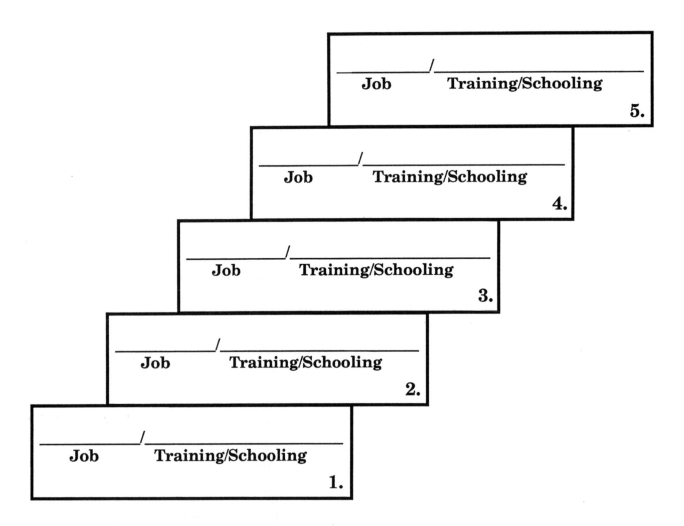

Job   /   Training/Schooling
5.

Job   /   Training/Schooling
4.

Job   /   Training/Schooling
3.

Job   /   Training/Schooling
2.

Job   /   Training/Schooling
1.

✎ Do the same "ladder" progression for another job.

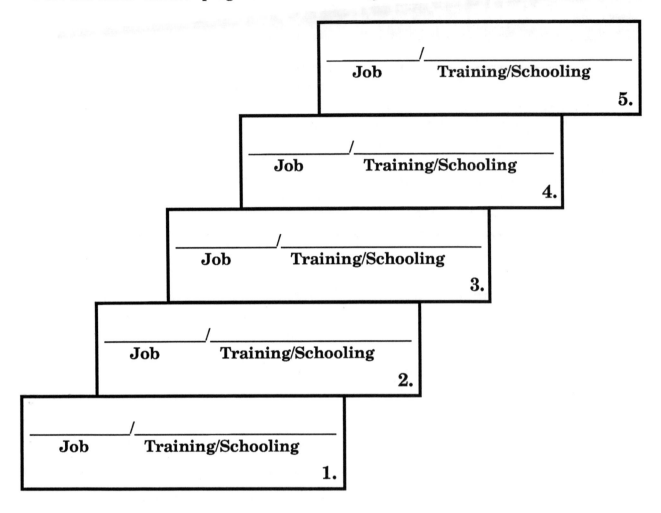

_____/_____
Job   Training/Schooling
5.

_____/_____
Job   Training/Schooling
4.

_____/_____
Job   Training/Schooling
3.

_____/_____
Job   Training/Schooling
2.

_____/_____
Job   Training/Schooling
1.

Thinking About This. *Starting with the first job, I will write the schooling needed at each level. I will begin by starting with the schooling I already have to get the first job at the related entry level up the ladder (i.e. 2 years at Washington High, beginning electronics). Do this for each level. Use this format and do this with three other jobs you could start right now.*

Sharing (Co-workers). *Discuss your explorations and thoughts about your job/career progression. Were you surprised that you really knew how you wanted to step up? Give feedback to help each member feel more secure about their plans. Discuss moving to different jobs at the same level (horizontal mobility).*

A CAREER FOR YOUR FUTURE

> ***Challenge.*** The ***Dictionary of Occupational Titles*** *lists thousands of career possibilities. It may be too early to decide on a definite career. You may wish to begin directing your discovered interests and abilities toward the courses and training you take and the activities you do outside of school.*
>
> *Many people begin to make money in their career choice early in life. For example, a person interested in landscape architecture may begin by taking care of lawns after school.*

Explore

✎ Use the ***Dictionary of Occupational Titles*** (and other reference materials) to find TWO careers/jobs that relate to your interests and abilities.

  1._____   2. _____

✎ Show how you can relate your "area of expertise" (abilities, interest, academic skills, etc.) with each career/job.

  1. Career/Job: _____

  _____

  _____

  _____

  _____

  _____

  2. Career/Job: _____

  _____

  _____

  _____

  _____

  _____

> ***Thinking About This.*** *I will make a career/job booklet with two chapters. Each chapter will have one of the careers I choose. I will research job descriptions, job availability, education and training needed, salaries, location of jobs, companies offering this career—including ideas on how to begin to become an expert. I will send for pamphlets, descriptions and answers to specific questions. I will visit the State Employment Service counselors, school counselors, and interview specialists in those job fields.*
>
> ***Sharing (Co-workers).*** *Team up with one other co-worker with a similar career to research. Assemble and present a written and oral report on this career/job choice. The co-worker and the Co-worker group will help you keep on track and on schedule. Important!! Work together with your group to make the project as easy, yet as complete as possible by designing a workable format, sharing research, responsibilities and delegating tasks.*

✎ Write your notes and suggestions given by others in the space below.

LEFT BRAIN—RIGHT BRAIN

> **Challenge.** *Your brain has many general functions or "rooms." You "own" all these rooms, but you may like to spend more time in certain ones, perhaps you have not visited some of them recently. The activities below will let you roam from room to room. Move comfortably through the following brain activities to discover your strengths and weaknesses in your left and right brain.*

Explore

✎ Invent eight new letters of the alphabet and explain how to say their phonetic sounds.

1. _____
2. _____
3. _____
4. _____
5. _____
6. _____
7. _____
8. _____

✎ Write two lines of lyrics to a new song.

1. _____
2. _____

✎ Hypothesize: Prove 2 + 2 does NOT equal 4. (Your logic doesn't have to make sense.)

_____
_____
_____

✎ Hypothesize: Prove 2 + 2 DOES equal 4.

_____
_____
_____

✎ Do something—anything in this space.

✎ Why does this figure appear 3 dimensional on a 2 dimensional page? (Explain without words to someone else until they understand.)

✎ Sketch a portrait of your leader UPSIDE DOWN. Then, do the same thing RIGHT SIDE UP.

NMOᗡ ƎᗡISԀ∩

RIGHT SIDE UP

✎ Which sketch is better? Why?

_____

_____

_____

_____

> ***Thinking About This.*** *What mood do I get into to do my best work? What is my best work? Why does that mood help? Where am I? Who am I with? What am I doing? How long can I keep it up? What do I do with my best work? What does this tell me about my interests? Aptitudes? Choice of classes? Training? Jobs? Careers? Friends? Co-workers? Mates? Am I directing my energy in a way that gives me "juice?" Is what I am doing draining me of energy? How can I change my mood (attitude) to do what I want in my present circumstances? What can I change in my environment? In others? How can I use what life gives me? How can I better serve others — using my "juice-producers." Am I more partial to the left or right side of my brain?*
>
> ***Sharing (Family).*** *Share your thoughts about your right- and left-brained strengths and your "juice-producers." Discuss each of your ideas from Thinking About This. Encourage the others to explore their strengths and not-so-strong areas. Do this with gentleness and insight. See your own insight.*

✎ Write about something you know absolutely nothing about. Sound like an expert!

There is absolutely no doubt in my mind that... _____

_____

_____

_____

_____

_____

_____

_____

_____

_____

_____

_____

_____

_____

_____

_____

_____

_____

THE PATH FROM HERE TO THERE

Challenge. (QUESTION) *Do you know why most Americans don't live in California?* (RESPONSE) *No, why?* (ANSWER) *They never made a decision to go and never made a plan to get there.*

Explore

✎ Explore new directions now!

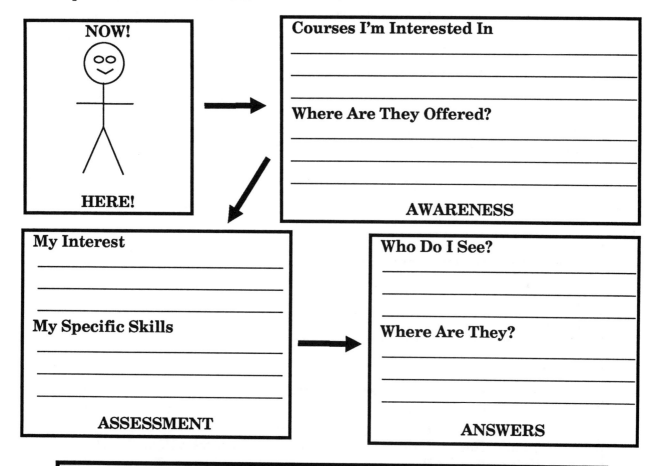

NOW!

HERE!

Courses I'm Interested In

_____

_____

_____

Where Are They Offered?

_____

_____

_____

_____

AWARENESS

My Interest

_____

_____

My Specific Skills

_____

_____

_____

ASSESSMENT

Who Do I See?

_____

_____

Where Are They?

_____

_____

_____

ANSWERS

Thinking About This. Am I part of a very specific plan? What is it? How am I doing? What do I need to do yet?

Sharing (Family). Share your goals and your paths with your Family. How specific should we be? Why? Do you have a California-type decision? Be even more specific. Now, get even more specific. How specific can you get?

SHOULD YOU BE THINKING ABOUT YOUR FUTURE?

> ***Challenge.*** *Most people try to foresee their future. For example, the author of this program just asked himself, "What will I be when I grow up?"*

Explore

✎ List some thoughts others think you "should" have about your future and rank them in levels of importance to you. (Number 1 being most important.)

(　　)＿＿＿＿＿＿＿＿＿＿＿＿＿＿＿＿＿＿＿＿＿＿＿＿＿＿＿

(　　)＿＿＿＿＿＿＿＿＿＿＿＿＿＿＿＿＿＿＿＿＿＿＿＿＿＿＿

(　　)＿＿＿＿＿＿＿＿＿＿＿＿＿＿＿＿＿＿＿＿＿＿＿＿＿＿＿

✎ List some kinds of schools or training that will be available to you in the next one to three years and rank these in order of importance.

(　　)＿＿＿＿＿＿＿＿＿＿＿＿＿＿＿＿＿＿＿＿＿＿＿＿＿＿＿

(　　)＿＿＿＿＿＿＿＿＿＿＿＿＿＿＿＿＿＿＿＿＿＿＿＿＿＿＿

(　　)＿＿＿＿＿＿＿＿＿＿＿＿＿＿＿＿＿＿＿＿＿＿＿＿＿＿＿

✎ Decide on three bits of information to find out about these schools. Then determine the order of research priority.

(　　)＿＿＿＿＿＿＿＿＿＿＿＿＿＿＿＿＿＿＿＿＿＿＿＿＿＿＿

(　　)＿＿＿＿＿＿＿＿＿＿＿＿＿＿＿＿＿＿＿＿＿＿＿＿＿＿＿

(　　)＿＿＿＿＿＿＿＿＿＿＿＿＿＿＿＿＿＿＿＿＿＿＿＿＿＿＿

> ***Thinking About This.*** *What are my most pressing decisions? How am I dealing with them? What are my options? Am I a worrier? Procrastinator? Over-Planner? Under-Planner? Flexible? Rigid? Do I seek options? Slide by? Wait? Wait for What? What is my plan for getting moving? Toward what? What is my goal? Goals? Plans? Action? Who decides? Why? How? When? What?*
>
> ***Sharing (Family).*** *Discuss the questions in Thinking About This with your Family. Be gentle! Brainstorm options. Discuss priorities. How are the challanges that others face similiar to yours? Different? Why? How? Share your most important decisions with the Community. Notice differences. Similarities.*

HOW I RELATE

> **Challenge.** *It would be nice if everybody always got along. But, most of our relationships change as we change. Living people have "alive" relationships. We go in and out and up and down in our relationships.*

Explore

✎ Think of some of your interactions with others. Circle the number that shows how the relationship is going at this time. Underline how you wish the relationship would go.

PERSON	POOR	GOOD	VERY GOOD
A close male friend	1	2	3
A close female friend	1	2	3
A distant male friend	1	2	3
A distant female friend	1	2	3
Most teachers	1	2	3
Most authorities	1	2	3
Religious authorities	1	2	3
Mother	1	2	3
Father	1	2	3
Sister	1	2	3
Brother	1	2	3
Grandmother	1	2	3
Grandfather	1	2	3
Other _____	1	2	3
Other _____	1	2	3
Other _____	1	2	3

✎ Pick a fictitious character with whom you are familiar (movies, books, T.V., etc.). Briefly tell about some of that person's ups and downs or ins and outs with others.

_____

_____

_____

_____

_____

_____

_____

_____

_____

_____

✎ Now choose a "real life" person you know. Tell of their fluctuating relationships.

_____

_____

_____

_____

_____

_____

_____

_____

_____

_____

_____

Thinking About This. *I have a friendship that is going very well. What do I do and think that makes it so good? I will think of a relationship that is going poorly and describe it. How can a poor relationship be made better?*

Sharing (Family). *Discuss your "good" and "poor" relationships. What is working? What doesn't? Should some relationships be stopped? Discuss. Who seems to be the hardest to get along with? Easiest? Hardest to understand? Easiest? Why? How? When? Why?*

SEEKER? FINDER?

> ***Challenge.*** *This is an age of seeking more, less; better, worse; higher, deeper; narrower, broader; more intense, less intense; heavier, lighter; etc., etc.*

Explore

✎ List five areas in which you are are "Seeking." Name its opposite.

SEEKING	ITS OPPOSITE
1. _____	_____
2. _____	_____
3. _____	_____
4. _____	_____
5. _____	_____

✎ Circle three of those that you think you can attain. List them below in order of importance and tell how you will be a "finder."

1. _____

_____

2. _____

_____

3. _____

_____

> ***Thinking About This.*** *What is best—being a seeker or a finder? Which one of the three I've listed above can I discard and still have a sense of fulfillment? Should I? Why? Have I left anything out?*
>
> ***Sharing (Friends).*** *Share your thoughts with your Friends. Listen close to the seeking and finding of others. How do others "find?" What is the feeling of finding "IT?" What is "IT?" Do you personally play a role in helping others be "finders?" How? When? Why? What is the feeling of being a habitual seeker without finding? Give examples.*

I AM GOOD

Challenge. *You are a loving, caring and sharing person.*

Explore

✎ Describe personal examples in your life where you demonstrated the following attributes.

Friendship: _____

_____

_____

Achievement: _____

_____

_____

Inner Harmony: _____

_____

_____

Wisdom: _____

_____

_____

Beauty: _____

_____

_____

Respect: _____

_____

_____

Accomplishment: _____

_____

_____

Freedom: _____

_____

_____

Security: _____

_____

_____

Transcendence: _____

_____

_____

Excitement: _____

_____

_____

Admiration: _____

_____

_____

Thinking About This. *Who sees (or has seen) me as a loving, caring, sharing person? What did they see in me? Do I accept that view as honest? Why? Why not? What do I need to do to be even more "upbeat" about myself? Do I want to be "good" always? Can I forgive my own humanness and failings? Should I? Why? When? How? Where? With whom?*

Sharing (Friends). *Share the examples where you demonstrated the qualities listed in Explore. Which attributes were new ideas to you? Describe the qualities that are the hardest to be. Explain. Why is it difficult to accept our own attributes? For each quality listed brainstorm its negative counterpart with your Family.*

MY DAY-TO-DAY LIFE

Challenge. *During most hours of the day you have both an obligation to others and a chance to give a gift to yourself that shows your loving and caring of yourself. The key to a successful day is your attitude of giving to yourself and others.*

Explore

✎ Fill in the grid showing your obligations and a "gift" you may receive at the same time.

TIME	MY OBLIGATION TO OTHERS	THE GIFT I MAY RECEIVE
6:00—8:00 a.m.		
8:00 a.m.-Noon		
Noon-4:00 p.m.		
4:00-8:00 p.m.		
8:00-Midnight		

Thinking About This. *Do I "give" to others? What? How? Why? What do I get in return from them? Can I feel good about myself even if the others don't give in return? How? How does giving to myself make me even more capable of sharing with others? Is there a balance? How do I achieve it?*

Sharing (Family). *Discuss your thoughts. Present your thoughts to the Community in a method of your choice (panel, teaching unit, skit, etc.).*

HUGGING

> **Challenge.** *Researchers have suggested that a person needs 10 or more hugs a day to survive and thrive in today's hectic world. Yet in some cultures hugs may be a violation of personal space.*

Explore

✎ It is not practical (I am told) to have an exercise in a book that encourages hugging. But, it would look and feel ridiculous to substitute handshakes for hugs. (They can be nice too, but not the same as a hug.) So, this is an exercise to prepare you to be hugged. Hugs must be extra-curricular activities (or you could be arrested for "hugstitution"). Complete the exercise below with examples of occasions when it is appropriate and not appropriate to hug someone.

	HUGGER	HUGGEE	MESSAGE SENT
Example:	Parent	Young Child	I approve of you, love you
Common:	1.		
	2.		
Sometimes:	1.		
	2.		
Never:	1.		
	2.		
Add two examples from your experience:	1.	Me	
	2. Me		

✎ List other ways to give someone a "huggy" type feeling.

Words to use

_____   _____

_____   _____

_____   _____

Sounds to make

_____   _____

_____   _____

_____   _____

Gifts that don't cost money

_____   _____

_____   _____

_____   _____

Thinking About This. What are the different messages hugs send? Can I get too old to be hugged? When? Who do I let hug me? Who do I hug? Have I made hugs only a part of dating? Can a hug be enjoyed just for itself? Who is missing not being hugged by me? Do animals have an equivilant of hugging? Give examples and what they must feel. Am I an animal? What kind? When? How? Is that OK?

Sharing (Family). Discuss all of the above with your Family members. Then, discuss the possibility of an on-campus hug (with gentleness, respect, dignity, what else?). Why? How? When? Why not?

THE MIND

Challenge. *"The mind is a wonderful tool when utilized fully."*

Explore

Bloom, a brilliant educator, devised a system of looking at our thinking process. He discovered levels of thinking that ranged from the simplest to the most complex. Your task is to research the dynamics of each level of the "Thinking Process" as they relate to an interest of yours.

✎ **Knowledge.** Think of your memory as a file system. Your task is to see general information as being in a mental filing system that you must bring out of your brain's file. Pick an interest about which you know a lot and recall eight simple facts about that interest.

1._____   5._____

2._____   6._____

3._____   7._____

4._____   8._____

✎ **Comprehension.** Research and define "comprehension."

_____

_____

_____

_____

✎ Write a statement showing that you comprehend two or three of the facts listed under "Knowledge" by combining them in a useful paragraph.

_____

_____

_____

_____

_____

_____

_____

_____

✎ **Application.** Use your key ideas, rules or principles described under "Knowledge" and "Comprehension" to match your interest with that of another person. (Example: How my interest in music can be combined with that of a friend who likes to teach preschoolers.)

_____

_____

_____

_____

_____

_____

_____

_____

✎ **Analysis.** Look closely at what you wrote under "Application." Break it down down into two or three of its main parts.

1. _____

_____

2. _____

_____

3. _____

_____

✎ **Synthesis.** Put together these parts from "Analysis" to make a whole that wasn't there before. (Example: A unique communication, a plan or discovery that builds from your thoughts.)

_____

_____

_____

_____

_____

_____

_____

✎ **Evaluation.** A standard is created with which to make judgements. An evaluation can be internal—consistent within itself. (Does it finish as good as it started?) Evaluations can also be external—comparing the work with outside criteria. (Another work similiar to your subject.)

✎ Evaluate the work that you did in each of sections. What is your method of judging?

Knowledge: _____

_____

Comprehension:_____

_____

Application: _____

_____

Analysis: _____

_____

Synthesis: _____

_____

Evaluation: _____

_____

Thinking About This. What parts of this lesson were the easiest for me? Hardest? Why? Can I work with my Family to clarify any of this lesson? How? Is it important that I understand it all? Why? Am I to be evaluated by how close to "perfect" I know the six points above? What do I feel? Think? I will make my own standards by which I am to be evaluated in this lesson and list them here.

Sharing (Co-workers). Discuss what was clear and was not clear in this lesson. What do you really want to learn about The Mind? What does the leader want from you in this lesson? How can you find out? Should you ignore what the author expected from you? How can you do that? What other options do you have? Could you rewrite this lesson on THE MIND so that it made more sense to you? Discuss this. Share your conclusions with the Community.

OFF THE CUFF

> **Challenge.** *You have a rare privilege. The members of the Community have given themselves to you for three minutes. That's right! You will have the complete attention of the group for three whole minutes. You must not plan or give anything "canned." When you get to the front you may teach, instruct or entertain. Or, just as important, you can ask what you want from the group.*
>
> *It is OK to be embarrassed or shy. Just explain these feelings. The KEY WORD of you for the group and the group toward you is "respect." Respect each other!*

Explore

✎ Before OFF THE CUFF begins, write your feelings about the task you are about to do.

_____

_____

_____

_____

_____

_____

_____

_____

✎ Do you feel you would rather prepare something? Why?

_____

_____

_____

_____

_____

_____

_____

_____

✎ What does it mean to "respect" the person who has your focus or attention?

_____

_____

_____

_____

✎ List three specific ways you can demonstrate this respect.

1. _____

2. _____

3. _____

✎ How can you show "respect" toward the Community when you have your three minutes?

_____

_____

_____

Thinking About This. *Was it hard for me to know I was going to direct the class in a few minutes, yet not think about it? For the next minute I will not think of anything—especially not of a good-looking person of the opposite gender. Beginning now I will not think of that gorgeous or handsome hunk of humanity. I will put this person out of my mind for one minute. I TRY this attempt now—for one minute. (The minute is up.) How did I do? Is it possible to use will power to force out a thought? Did I manage to not nurture a thought or does trying to force one out only intensify it? Why does the word "try" imply failure? How about the word "attempt?" What other words are implied failure words?*

Sharing (Family). *How did it get to be OFF THE CUFF? Did you plan—even if the rules said "No?" Share this with your Family. Why? How? Is it impossible not to? Why? Discuss the implied failure words and how they are used.*

SIMULATION I— OUR FAMILY PROBLEM

A member of your Family has a troubling problem that threatens his/her life. And, because you are a close Family each of your lives are delicately interwoven with this Family member. What YOU feel and think affects that person with the problem and what he/she experiences directly or indirectly is changing your life.

Your Family is not prepared to deal with a problem of this magnitude! You must have Family discussions to focus on the problem and to confront the issues that emerge from the problem.

There will be Family "pow-wows." The members with the problem must be absent from these pow-wows. (These "problem members" will meet in their own group to discuss their problems, how it affects their Families and to get support, comfort and professional help for themselves.)

The Family will seek help in the REAL local community in the form of doctors, counselors, addiction specialists, social workers, Hospice care, juvenile workers, etc. etc. WHATEVER it takes to go through this crisis!

WORKSHEET FOR OUR FAMILY PROBLEM

The problem we face is:_____
_____
_____
_____
_____
_____

The Family member with the problem is:_____
_____
_____
_____
_____
_____

The roles we are assuming for the Simulation:

✎ Father   ✎ Sister   Other: _____

✎ Mother   ✎ Brother   Other: _____

✎ Step-Father   ✎ Step-Brother

✎ Step-Mother   ✎ Step-Sister

✎ Define the specific problem (come to a clear group definition of a specific problem). Assume your own role and explain and play it FULLY! The conflicts the member's problem is causing ME—specifically!

_____

_____

_____

_____

✎ My loving feeling toward the member.

_____

_____

_____

_____

✎ What I would like to do if I had "magic."

_____

_____

_____

_____

✎ What I can realistically do—since I do not have "magic."

_____

_____

_____

_____

✎ What I think our Family should do in this situation.

_____

_____

_____

_____

✎ Now, I will get with my Family to begin to discuss the problem and the alternatives, the plan of action and our next step. Use additional "JOURNALING" to document your corrective steps, share your feelings and thoughts, etc.

SELF-INVENTORY I

> ***Challenge.*** *I will evaluate myself. How am I doing so far? Before I begin answering these questions, I will review my responses in Section I and what I have learned about myself.*

Explore

✎ I will ask myself these questions honestly and with a fair degree of self-examination.

CHARACTERISTIC	CIRCLE ONE		
	LOW		HIGH
My Level of Sincerity			
Desire to do my best.....................	1	2	3
Attempt to learn more	1	2	3
Wish to cooperate	1	2	3
My Research			
Use of many sources.....................	1	2	3
Clear, straight-forward responses.................	1	2	3
Attempt to find more resources.................	1	2	3
My Awareness of Self			
Discovering new things	1	2	3
Desire to improve	1	2	3
Working on personal challenges	1	2	3
My Awareness of Others			
Cooperation in groups	1	2	3
Level of ability to communicate ideas.............	1	2	3
Ability to assist others.....................	1	2	3
My Written and Oral Products			
Quality of oral reports	1	2	3
Excellence of written work.....................	1	2	3
Amount of preparation for work	1	2	3
The Carry-over Outside School			
Homework.....................	1	2	3
Degree of interest in my studies	1	2	3
Hobbies and interests that relate	1	2	3
Overall Sense of Personal Satisfaction			
My satisfaction in my personal growth...........	1	2	3
Ability to increase my friendships.................	1	2	3
Amount of available energy used	1	2	3
Degree progressed toward my potential	1	2	3

FAMILY INVENTORY I

Challenge. *I will now evaluate my Family honestly and lovingly.*

Explore

✎ Now that you have completed the first Simulation in this book, express your opinions about your Family. Think carefully how your Family worked together.

CHARACTERISTIC	CIRCLE ONE		
	LOW		HIGH
Level Of Sincerity			
Our desire to do our best	1	2	3
Our attempt to learn more	1	2	3
Comments: _____			
Research			
Use of many sources	1	2	3
Clear, straight-forward sharing	1	2	3
Comments: _____			
Awareness			
Our attempt to listen to others' ideas	1	2	3
Effectiveness of Family communication	1	2	3
Comments: _____			
Cooperation			
Level at which we worked together	1	2	3
Our understanding of others' needs	1	2	3
Comments: _____			
Products			
Completion of our work	1	2	3
Clarity of our work	1	2	3
Appearance of our work	1	2	3
Comments: _____			

✎ I will use this format to make entries into my Journal to evaluate: 1) my Friends, 2) Co-workers, and 3) the Community.

MOVING ON

I have discovered much about myself in Section I. I have bonded with a Family and experienced the traumas of a member's major life problem and how it affected our Family.

I have also explored my participation in schooling, training and job/career possibilities. I have shared ideas with Co-workers and Friends and have expanded my inner circle of Family, Friends and Co-workers to include the larger community. I have shared with all of them. I can sense to what degree I have included them in my world. I can intuit to what degree each of them has opened up to me. And they sense the level of interaction I have allowed of myself with them.

I trust that my present level of involvement is what is comfortable to me. Interaction is a dance—I change my distances and degrees of involvement as the dance progresses. It is my privilege how, to what degree and when I do it! No one can make me or "grade" me on my "comfort zone." They can invite me in and hold me away. I can choose to get closer or to stay away. That's the dance!

In Section II, I will be making more decisions regarding my life:

✎ *Further training/schooling*

✎ *Opinions about life*

✎ *Looking "into" myself for qualities as a possible mate*

✎ *Making decisions and choices for potential life partners.*

© 1992, JIST Works, Inc. • Indianapolis, Indiana

SECTION II

Be Whatever You Want to Be

Perhaps our continuing journey brought us to this world—abruply. We were indignant because we were suddenly forced to adjust to a harsh environment. But we have survived and our journey continues as we constantly make decisions that enrich our lives.

Some decisions we make are very good and we enjoy the outcomes. Other decisions are not-so-good and we learn from our mistakes, grow in wisdom and strength and benefit from the experience. At times we are dependent, other times independent but always sensing our inner-dependence.

Now, we will learn even more about ourselves and others as we explore careers, discover our needs and find ways to best fulfill them. You will have a special friend, a "Mate," to explore the enriching experience of partnering. Together with Family, Friends, Co-workers and Mates, we will discuss and research lifestyles, planning, budgeting and communication skills.

Your classroom journey (and it is my hope your life journey as well) can only be complete when sensing satisfaction from cooperating with others. Not because you are inadequate alone, but because together we are more than just one plus one. We are a unit—a team—traveling together toward our goals and aspirations.

WORK HARD AND PLAY MUCH

Challenge. *Most of us are busy, busy, busy—like ants on a hill. Our brains even scurry about when we try to relax.*

Explore

✎ Write beside each activity your usual time spent. (Include each class, lunch, play, hobbies, TV, etc.)

ACTIVITY	HOURS/MINUTES
Getting ready for school/work	
Going to and coming from school/work	
Attending school/work	
Studying for school/work	
Reading for enjoyment	
Participating in hobbies and other interests	
Socializing with family/friends/co-workers	
Sleeping	
Eating meals	
Performing chores	
Other:	
Other:	
(should total 24 hours)	

Thinking About This. How would I change this schedule to better suit me? When am I too busy? Not busy enough? Not satisfied? Very satisfied?

Sharing (Friends). Share your schedules. Role play how your differing schedules create conflicts within your families. Work out satisfying and loving compromises or alternatives. What is the difference between the two? Which works best? When? How? Why? Role play, demonstrating each. Share your best play situation with the Community.

THINK OF THAT!

> **Challenge.** *The human body has 100 trillion cells. Each cell has enough information on its DNA so that if each piece of information was a word the information would fill 1,000 volumes. Now consider this! The "brain" library has 10,000 times more capacity than the "gene" library. Since the brain has 100 billion neurons there are 100 billion x 1,000 volumes or 100 trillion neural complexes. Each neural complex can handle multiple inter-relationships.*
>
> *Do you get the feeling from this that we are built to learn? It is impossible for us NOT to learn.*

Explore

✎ Everything that you have ever experienced is stored away for possible retrieval. Relax. Take three deep breaths and drift back in time. Allow your mind to float into nice pleasant thoughts from years ago. Read each of the following words. Write about the things that pop into your mind.

A birthday party:_____

_____

_____

_____

A broken bicycle: _____

_____

_____

_____

A neighbor's pet: _____

_____

_____

_____

A mean and ornery story character: _____

_____

_____

_____

A loving touch: _____

_____

_____

_____

A scoop of delicious ice cream: _____

_____

_____

_____

A special teacher or mentor: _____

_____

_____

_____

Thinking About This. *My mind is in constant activity. I will use my journal to jot down strings of words as they pop into my mind. I won't analyze or think. I will just write...write...write...*

Sharing (Friends). *Sit with your Friends in a circle. Each person is to start a word and the next person says a word that pops into their consciousness. (There are no right or wrong words.) Keep going around and around. Be aware of "connections." Some will be obvious, some obscure and some humorous. What other feelings were expressed during this experience? Talk about them. Pick two words that were said in a row (example, horse-paper). Go around the circle free-associating by linking words that MAY HAVE fit in between those two words to form a connection. (Example, shoe-fly, or horse-shoe-fly-paper.)*

© 1992, JIST Works, Inc. • Indianapolis, Indiana

BIAS

Challenge. I liked that person right away!

Explore

✎ How would you define bias?

_____

_____

_____

_____

_____

_____

✎ Brainstorm four examples where bias could interfere with logical thinking.

1. _____

_____

2. _____

_____

3. _____

_____

4. _____

_____

✎ You are researching a chemical formula for the cure of cancer. How will bias interfere with your findings?

_____

_____

_____

_____

_____

✎ List two ways that you have exhibited bias in the last five days.

1. _____

_____

_____

2. _____

_____

_____

✎ In what ways are bias and prejudice the same? Give some examples.

_____

_____

_____

_____

_____

_____

✎ In what ways are bias and prejudice different? Give some examples.

_____

_____

_____

_____

_____

_____

Thinking About This. *How is having bias an advantage? Disadvantage? When do I use bias to my advantage? Disadvantage? Should I think differently? How? When?*

Sharing (Friends). *Brainstorm ways bias exhibits itself in school. At home. In our personal lives. What are ways to avoid or overcome bias? Plan a short skit demonstrating bias and how it can create understanding.*

IMPORTANT DECISIONS

> ***Challenge.*** *Most people are making their own decisions on such matters as family, religion, lifestyle, education, career and goals.*

Explore

✎ These statements are definite opinions from young adults. Notice your reaction to the statements and write what you think about each. Rewrite the statement in your own opinion.

I believe every person should make their OWN decisions.

_____

_____

_____

_____

_____

_____

_____

Being happy is more important than making money.

_____

_____

_____

_____

_____

_____

_____

Most people will do better if pushed.

_____

_____

_____

_____

_____

_____

_____

Traditional marriage must be strengthened to save the family.

_____

_____

_____

_____

_____

_____

Everyone should feel a responsibility to serve their country.

_____

_____

_____

_____

_____

_____

_____

The family is becoming the strong and important unit it once was.

_____

_____

_____

_____

_____

_____

Thinking About This. *What do I feel really strongly about? Why? When? How do I express it in my life? How does this affect my life? Other's lives? What if I am wrong? Can I be? Why? How? When?*

Sharing (Family). *Share each revised opinion with your family. Discuss differences while honoring the opinions of the others.*

PRESENT YOUR VIEWPOINT

> ***Challenge.*** *You have taken a stand on certain key issues. You are now asked to defend your position or viewpoint.*

Explore

✎ On the previous page you stated that you believed that....

_____

_____

_____

_____

_____

_____

_____

_____

✎ Find three or four other persons (Co-workers) who felt strongly the same way.

Person:_____

Viewpoint:_____

_____

Person:_____

Viewpoint:_____

_____

Person:_____

Viewpoint:_____

_____

Person:_____

Viewpoint:_____

_____

✎ Prepare to present your viewpoint to the Community. Brainstorm about the ideas. Then, rank that supportive material and make an appropriate list. Proceed as follows:

Plan for developing the presentation.

_____

_____

_____

_____

_____

_____

Gather materials, facts, figures, illustrations, etc. that you will need.

_____

_____

_____

_____

_____

_____

✎ Assign responsibilities.

NAME	RESPONSIBILITY

Thinking About This. Was it hard to find someone who shares my viewpoint? Do we agree on every aspect of that viewpoint? Did the Community accept or reject our viewpoint? Did they respect or "inspect" our viewpoint?

Sharing (Community). Share with the Community what you learned about each group's viewpoint. Could you see their point? Why? Was it hard to listen to their point if you didn't agree? Why?

MAJOR CHOICES TO MAKE IN LIFE

Challenge. *We have to make choices from birth to death. Some choices are easy to make—other choices are harder and more difficult to make. Some decisions seem almost impossible to make.*

Explore

✎ List three choices that a person might have to make at different ages in life. Decide if the level of difficulty for each choice is easy or hard.

AGE	THE THREE CHOICES	LEVEL/DIFFICULTY
Birth to 5	1.	
	2.	
	3.	
6 to 11	1.	
	2.	
	3.	
12 to 15	1.	
	2.	
	3.	
16 to 20	1.	
	2.	
	3.	
20 to 40	1.	
	2.	
	3	
40 to 60	1.	
	2.	
	3.	
Over 60	1.	
	2.	
	3.	

✎ Now your task is to list five choices that you have already made. Share the outcome that you experienced and the level of difficulty for each.

1. _____

_____

_____

2. _____

_____

_____

3. _____

_____

_____

4. _____

_____

_____

5. _____

_____

_____

Thinking About This. *What is my definition of easy? Hard? Who decides to make it easy? Hard? What is my attitude toward easy things? Hard choices? Hard work? Hard relationships?*

Sharing (Family). *What makes the difference between easy and hard? When is it easy to think? Feel? Sense? Perceive? Make decisions? When is it hard?*

UNDERSTANDING THE FULL IMPLICATIONS

> **Challenge.** *You are to be a participant in the following situations. Tell what you would do.*

Explore

✎ A person begins to choke on food in a restaurant.

_____

_____

_____

_____

✎ You have only five minutes to prepare before describing your academic plans to the community.

_____

_____

_____

_____

✎ You find out that toxic chemicals are being absorbed into your water system.

_____

_____

_____

_____

✎ A car is approaching a washed-out bridge.

_____

_____

_____

_____

✎ A local factory created an acid rain that removed paint from your new car.

_____

_____

_____

_____

✎ A neighbor is abusing their pet.

_____

_____

_____

_____

✎ A neighbor is abusing your pet.

_____

_____

_____

_____

✎ A friend with three young children is driving a car with defective brakes.

_____

_____

_____

_____

✎ Your place of worship has suffered damage in a fire and needs money to rebuild.

_____

_____

_____

_____

✎ Your friend is doing poorly in school.

_____

_____

_____

_____

✎ A young woman just slapped a child in the booth next to you.

_____

_____

_____

_____

✎ Your neighbor is a public official, who you know uses drugs.

_____

_____

_____

_____

✎ A friend is your neighbor. You know this friend does drugs.

_____

_____

_____

_____

> ***Thinking About This.*** *How do I handle tough decisions? Am I good in an emergency? When has someone depended on me and I helped? Have I let anyone down? Saved a life? Made someone's life better? How can I do even better? Am I too hard on myself? In what way?*
>
> ***Sharing (Friends).*** *Share your thoughts and feelings in Thinking About This. Discuss the way you would handle each situation in Explore. Be aware of even better responses than your own. Express yourself clearly and simply.*

THE INNER URGE—AND WHAT TO DO ABOUT IT

Challenge. *When very relaxed and quiet you can sometimes "hear" or "see" your thoughts. Some thoughts may sound just like what someone has said to you—even the tone of voice. A few of these may be upsetting or disturbing. Other thoughts are peaceful or very positive. These give clues as to what decisions to make, what projects to get into or what new directions to take in our lives. It is said that a person is blind until getting IN-sight. We are deaf until we hear that gentle, inner voice.*

Explore

✎ List three of your HONEST thoughts that create a nice feeling.

THOUGHT	THE FEELING
1. _____	
_____	
_____	_____
2. _____	
_____	
_____	_____
3. _____	
_____	
_____	_____

✎ Put to words, three of your HONEST thoughts that sound or look like they might have come from someone you know.

THOUGHT	WHO FROM
1. _____	
_____	
_____	_____
2. _____	
_____	
_____	_____
3. _____	
_____	
_____	_____

✎ List three of your HONEST thoughts that come from you directed to someone else.

THOUGHT	TO WHOM
1._____	
_____	
_____	_____
2._____	
_____	
_____	_____
3._____	
_____	
_____	

Thinking About This. *I will say each of the following words several times until I can "hear" or "see" my thoughts. Example: Friends ... Friends ... Friends ... until the thoughts slow and I jot them down. Friends. Training. Schooling. Career. Job. Partner. Family. Hobbies. Interests.*

Sharing (Family). *Compare your thoughts with that of other Family members. Who is right? Wrong? How are your thoughts different? The same?*

Discuss the factors that brought us to your way of thinking. Are we changing? Can we? Should we? How? When? Why?

NEEDS AND CHOICES

> **Challenge.** *"I need you. I want you. I can't live without you. I don't need you or want you and I can live nicely without you, thank you. No, I think I want you for a not-to-close friend, but not 'too' distant would also be nice." We all have wants and needs, but which is which? Does it matter when making important decisions?*

Explore

✎ What is a "want?" (Dictionary definition.)

Want: _____

_____

_____

✎ What is a "need?" (Dictionary definition.)

Need: _____

_____

_____

✎ How can you personally tell the difference? Give an example using a want and a need in your own life.

_____

_____

_____

✎ We attempt to make choices in our lives that somehow satisfy our needs. Some needs are listed. Your task is to decide which choices in life fulfill these needs. (See example.) Numbers 1 — 5 are Maslow's "Hierarchy of Basic Needs." The rest are more general.

NEEDS	LIFE CHOICES
Example: Food/Elimination	Hunt, Fish ,"Nature Calls,"
1. Safety/Shelter	
2. Belonging	
3. Love	
4. Self-Actualize	

NEEDS	LIFE CHOICES
5. Relieve Anxiety	
6. Support	
7. Play	
8. Plan	
9. Proliferate	
10. Unity	
11. Morality	
12. Knowledge	
13. Go	
14. Handle Trauma	
15. Be Heard	
16. Be Seen	
17. Achieve	
18. Dependence	
19. Independence	
20. Inner-Dependence	
21. Other	
22. Other	

Thinking About This. Do I really have all these needs? Which ones seem new to me? Strange? Ridiculous? Am I a needy person? Why? Why not? How can I fulfill more needs? Should I? Why? Why not? Should I think about needs and wants? What are my options?

Sharing (Family). Can we be too introspective? What happens when we are? How can we switch our focus so that recognizing our own needs helps us understand what others are looking for? Let's plan on doing something to meet another person's need. Can it be done without that person knowing who did it and why? Why does meeting another's need satisfy us? What does this statement mean: Every behavior I see is someone either GIVING love or someone ASKING for love. How can that be true? Give examples from your own life and what you have observed.

SECURITY

> **Challenge.** *Everyone who sells something wants you to feel a NEED for their product or service. Their formula is this: 1) To make you aware of an inner lack, 2) To show you that their product fills that lack in others, and 3) To convince you that your need can be filled with what they are selling.*

Explore

✎ Do you want to be like the persons in the ads who demonstrated security through owning? How are your needs the SAME as others? Different?

SAME NEEDS	DIFFERENT NEEDS
1. A house	
2. A pet	
3. A car	
4. Life insurance	
5. A funeral policy	
6. Designer jeans	

✎ List five important products or services that give the satisfaction or fulfillment that they promise. What need does each fulfill?

PRODUCT	NEED IT FULFILLS
1. _____	_____
_____	_____
_____	_____
2. _____	_____
_____	_____
_____	_____
3. _____	_____
_____	_____
_____	_____
4. _____	_____
_____	_____
_____	_____
5. _____	_____
_____	_____
_____	_____

✎ Where is your security? Explain.

_____

_____

_____

_____

_____

_____

✎ When you let go of everything—what is left? Explain.

_____

_____

_____

_____

_____

_____

✎ Now, a ruthless dictator tells you to let go of that! What is left? Amplify this response.

_____

_____

_____

_____

_____

_____

_____

✎ Now, let go of it. What is left?

_____

_____

_____

_____

_____

Thinking About This. *What do I want now? How do I get it? Where? When? Why?*

Sharing (Family). *Share your semi-necessary needs with your Family. What makes you happy? Sad? Satisfied? Loving? What brings enjoyment? What IS enjoyment? How does a person "grow" personally? Discuss areas where you have grown. Is growth easy? What is MOST needful? What are "spiritual" needs? How are they fulfilled?*

PERSONAL GROWTH

> **Challenge.** *"Growth takes place when the next step forward is subjectively more delightful, more joyous, more intrinsically satisfying than the previous gratification with which we have become familiar and even bored."*
> —*Abraham Maslow*

Explore

✎ Rewrite Maslow's idea about GROWTH in your own words.

_____

_____

_____

_____

_____

_____

_____

✎ List four personal experiences in your life when you "grew" after being bored, over-familiar, or in personal pain.

1. _____

_____

_____

2. _____

_____

_____

3. _____

_____

_____

4. _____

_____

_____

✎ Share these experiences with your Family members.

_____
_____
_____
_____
_____
_____
_____

> ***Thinking About This.*** *How do I know when I "grow." Why did I? Why should I? Can I make someone else change? Who decides what changes I should make? Does anyone else have a say-so in getting me to change? What if I am doing something that hurts me? Hurts them? Can I change? What about me will probably never change? What in me resists change? What do I respect in people who try to get me to change? Resent? What methods does each use?*
>
> ***Sharing (Family).*** *Design a working definition of "personal growth" that everyone in your Family agrees on. What changes are necessary in a family? What is hardest to change? Share your personal experiences of changes as listed above. Go into as much detail as you feel comfortable.*

MY QUALITIES AS A POSSIBLE MATE

> **Challenge.** *I bring ME into this union of one person seeking to be with you in a closer, more intimate way. I have more than my body to offer to you. In fact, many things about me make me unique and valuable to you. Though my body is more similiar to others, WHO I AM and what I DESIRE TO GIVE is what makes me different.*

Explore

✎ You have listed your assets, gifts, aptitudes and qualities to bring into schooling, training, jobs, careers, etc. Now, you have an opportunity to list the PERSONAL qualities that make you valuable as a possible mate. (Not physical, financial or tangible "stuff.")

_____

_____

_____

_____

_____

_____

_____

_____

_____

✎ List 8 qualities that you want in a mate. (Not physical, financial or tangible "stuff.")

1. _____
2. _____
3. _____
4. _____
5. _____
6. _____
7. _____
8. _____

✎ Which qualities in me match (are compatible) with those I want in a mate?

MY QUALITIES	MATE'S QUALITIES
_____	_____
_____	_____
_____	_____
_____	_____
_____	_____
_____	_____

✎ Write a definition of "compatibility" and how it relates to the quality matching you just completed.

_____

_____

_____

_____

_____

_____

_____

_____

_____

_____

Thinking About This. *I will check (✔) my best four traits above. Why do I think these are my best? I will tell of times when I exhibit these qualities that would assit me in being a good mate. What are the four "best" qualities that I want a mate to exhibit? Why? When? How? What about my traits I didn't check makes them not as "good?" What can I do to improve in those? (Write a plan.) What one or two more would I add to become an even better mate?*

Sharing (Family). *Discuss what mates need and want. What qualities do each of you have that makes you desirable mates (nonphysical or material). Make a skit demonstrating some quality "mate" characteristics. Ask the Community to tell what traits you demonstrated in your skit.*

IMPORTANT!

> **Challenge.** *"I LOVE YOU!" (What does that mean—really?)*

Explore

✎ Research suggests that successful partners have as their first three qualities those listed below. Your task is to list some other attributes you feel are in good relationships and give an example for each. (*Hint:* Think of some not-so-good characteristics in a poor relationship and find the opposite.)

QUALITY	AN EXAMPLE
1. Loving	
2. Caring	
3. Sharing	
4. Sense of Humor	
5. Good Communication	
6.	
7.	
8.	
9.	
10.	

✎ Give further examples in your own life when you (or others) demonstrated the following actions:

Loving:_____

_____

Caring:_____

_____

Sharing:_____

_____

Humor: _____

_____

Communicating: _____

_____

Other:_____

_____

Other:_____

_____

Thinking About This. *I will write my thoughts about each of the qualities given in numbers 1-5. Then I will write about five of my own suggestions in numbers 6-10. I will soon be assigned to a mate or to a temporary single life. How do I feel about this? Which do I REALLY prefer now?*

Sharing (Mate/Family/Community). *Share your qualities of good partnering and list each one on the board (check when it is stated more than once to get a tally). Rank order your Community's priorities and discuss them. Use a "panel of experts" to discuss each quality. Invite outside authorities on the subject (ie., marriage counselors, sociologists, etc.).*

CAREERS

Challenge. *Your career choice shapes your personal and academic choices. It deserves your best effort.*

Explore

✎ Plan a field trip to your local employment service (or arrange for a job expert to visit your class). Perhaps you can take the aptitude and interest test batteries to assist you in determining your career aptitudes and interests. Use the *Dictionary of Occupational Titles* or *Encyclopedia of Occupational Choices* to list four careers that you may enjoy. Research the necessary schooling and the yearly salaries.

CAREER	SCHOOL REQUIREMENTS	SALARY RANGE IN 19☐

✎ Now, imagine that you are a personnel manager seeking applicants for these four
career choices. Write a newspaper ad for each opening.

Ad #1:_____

_____

_____

_____

_____

_____

_____

Ad #2:_____

_____

_____

_____

_____

_____

_____

Ad #3:_____

_____

_____

_____

_____

_____

_____

Ad #4:_____

_____

_____

_____

_____

_____

_____

 © 1992, JIST Works, Inc. • Indianapolis, Indiana

✎ Write an ad as if you are looking for a job. Describe your assets and interests.

My ad: _____

_____

_____

_____

_____

_____

_____

✎ Have a Family member write an ad for you describing your assets and interests.

_____

_____

_____

_____

_____

_____

_____

Thinking About This. *Do I really want to think of careers and my future now? Why? Why not? What pressure is on me? Do I like the pressure? Do I wish I had more pressure on me? What can others do to give me what I need in the way of support? How do support and pressure differ? How are they the same? Can someone be supportive but I feel it as pressure? How do I feel about all the tests and explorations? Is there a better way for me to discover my skills? Am I assisting others in my Family and Co-workers group? Who in the groups are helful to me? What is it they do that helps? Can I let them know? Is it time to get over the self-consciousness of being "read" and candid? How? Why should I?*

Sharing (Family). *Discuss each introspective question in Thinking and those you added on your own. What happens when you share openly and honestly?*

WAGES AND WORKERS

Challenge. *A wage is the financial payoff for work. Personal satisfaction is the non-tangible reward.*

Explore

✎ Research the trend in wages for three occupations of interest to you. (Ask parents, neighbors, librarians, employers, etc.)

OCCUPATION	25 YEARS AGO	15 YEARS AGO	10 YEARS AGO	NOW	5 YEARS HENCE
1.					
2.					
3.					

✎ What must heavy industry workers plan for? Discuss.

_____

_____

_____

_____

✎ What is happening to the emphasis on producing "things?"

_____

_____

_____

_____

✎ Describe the trend toward high technology/service occupations.

_____

_____

_____

_____

✎ Why is the concept of management working WITH labor essential? How can it be done effectively? Give examples of a true "union."

_____

_____

_____

_____

_____

_____

_____

_____

_____

__Thinking About This.__ What kind of work do I like? Am I a factory type? Executive? A loner? Service oriented? What interests me? What am I good at? What job could I do right now and go up the ladder? What is a dead end? What is the relationship I want with authority—be my own boss? What is the corporate ladder? What about vocational training? Do I really need a college degree? One or both? Neither? High School diploma? What ARE other options open to me? Night school? How can I make options available? Do I spend more time picking out clothes or cars than my life decisions?

How can I learn more? How much will I tolerate to get my goals? If staying in the school/training is too hard what are other options? Do my priorities need adjustment? Are they in good, workable positions? What is my next step toward personal fulfillment? What is "success"—really? What does it mean that I am NOW a success by just accepting an attitude of success? Does that help me or make me lazy and complacent? How can I decide that I am NOW successful? I will decide I am NOW successful (this moment) and enjoy that feeling for awhile.

__Sharing (Co-workers).__ Discuss your Thinking thoughts. Be open—let ideas flow without judgement or restriction. Look at all options. Explore ways to develop the "I Am Already Successful" attitude.

Share your best ideas with the Community using the panel format (presenting ideas and fielding questions afterward).

CITY BUS

> **Challenge.** *It is very hard for most of us to separate our observations of what we see going on around us from our values (what we think and feel is important to us).*

Explore

✎ You will see a drawing of several people on a city bus. Something is happening. What is happening in this scene?

_____

_____

_____

_____

_____

✎ Who is the "hero?" Explain.

_____

_____

_____

_____

_____

✎ Who is the "bad" person? Explain.

_____

_____

_____

_____

_____

✎ What are each of these people thinking? Feeling?

The man and old lady: _____

_____

_____

_____

_____

The lady with the baby: _____

_____

_____

_____

_____

The religious-looking man: _____

_____

_____

_____

_____

The little guy bent over: _____

_____

_____

_____

_____

The two people with their backs to us: _____

_____

_____

_____

_____

✎ What do you see in this scene that bothers you?

_____

_____

_____

_____

_____

✎ What in the scene makes you feel good?

_____

_____

_____

_____

_____

✎ How would you change this scene if you could?

_____

_____

_____

_____

_____

_____

Thinking About This. Will the others see this scene close to the way that I see it? How else could it be seen? What is influencing my perceptions? Will I be able to change the minds of others?

Sharing (Family). What do other members of your group feel/think is happening in this scene? Try to make others agree with your interpretation. Discuss the differences of opinion. Be sure to attempt to see it THEIR way. Who is right? What is a "concept?" Give an example. What is a "pre-conception?" Example: Remember the bias and prejudice exercise?

HUH?

> ***Challenge.*** *I can't hear what you are saying. I am too busy listening for what I want to hear.*

Explore

✎ Write something that you would like your Mate, Family and the Community to know about you.

_____

_____

_____

_____

_____

_____

_____

_____

> ***Sharing (Mate/Family).*** *Share this information with your Mate or Family. Ask your Mate or one of your Family members to tell you, in detail, what you wanted them to know. Amplify your information to them until that person fully knows what you said. Now, switch giving and receiving information. Each Mate or member of every Family will share with the Community the information given to them by the other member.*

✎ Write something else that you want your Mate and/or Family to know about you. This information will NOT be shared with the Community.

_____

_____

_____

_____

_____

_____

_____

_____

✎ Finish these sentences:

"You would really be surprised and glad to know that I ... _____

_____

_____

_____

_____

_____

_____

"I've saved the best for last. It makes me proud to tell you that ... _____

_____

_____

_____

_____

_____

_____

_____

***Thinking About This.** I will write my feelings about being heard correctly. Was the information I gave passed on correctly and with respect by the other member? How? Why? What would I do differently next time regarding being heard correctly? Regarding listening and passing on the information that I was given?*

***Sharing (Mate/Family).** Tell what you want your Mates and Family to know. Is this different than the Explore exercise? In what way?*

AS THE WORLD CHURNS

> ***Challenge.*** *We all play different roles in a day. We act as students, friends, employees, sons and daughters. Those we meet also act out their roles.*

Explore

✎ Each Family will make a "Spin-a-Scene" board. Choose a director to spin to get: **A)** the scene (Home, Work, School, or Other, **B)** How many will act? (2, 3, 4 or 5) and **C)** The outcome (Good or Not-So-Good). The director will assign the characters and feelings to the actors and set the stage for the total scene.
Each member will take a turn being the director.

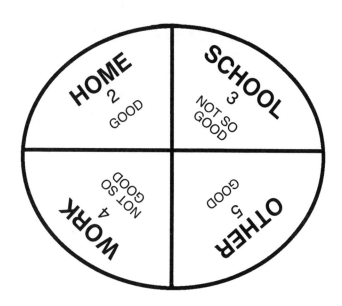

> ***Thinking About This.*** *What feelings do I have about the characters I played and how I played them? Do I really think that way? How would I really handle that in "real" life? Who do I know that is like these characters? How would they handle these situations? What role did I like doing best? Why? What roles didn't I like? Why? How would I have done the roles differently?*
>
> ***Sharing (Family).*** *Discuss your roles played. Share your best scene with the Community.*

TWO NEEDS INTERACTING

> **Challenge.** *You usually have a need working in you. Needs are physical (food, shelter, etc.), emotional (feeling wanted or wanting to give), or spiritual (being yourself fully). When you are with someone else they also have a need to fill or a need to express themselves. They hope to do it in some satisfying way. Both of you will have a satisfying time if you each get your need satisfied. You may feel unpleasant or uncomfortable if your needs go unfulfilled.*

Explore

✎ List some needs that you might have during the day. Then, give a need of another person that matches your need. (See examples.)

	NEEDS	NEEDS OF ANOTHER	WHO
Physical	To eat	To provide for the family	Parent
Physical			
Physical			
Emotional	To be comforted	To say nice things	Friend
Emotional			
Emotional			
Spriitual	To be creative	To teach art or music	Instructor
Spriitual			
Spriitual			

✎ List six more needs you have and how you satisfy each.

THE NEED	HOW I SATISFY THE NEED
1.	
2.	
3.	
4.	
5.	
6.	

Thinking About This. When do my needs directly conflict with needs of another? With whom does this happen? When? How do we resolve it? I will share with my Family an unresolved conflict and hear how they handle similiar situations.

Sharing (Family). Share your needs—both similiar ones and differing needs. Listen to unmet needs and discuss what can be done. Really hear! Give a hug and "thanks."

DEAR GABBY

> **Challenge.** *I really like your opinions and advice—especially if you agree with me. It makes me feel good to know that I am not alone.*

Explore

✎ It may be helpful to hear how other people solve problems. Write two problems on a sheet of paper that you would like answered. They can be your past or possible future, personal, schooling or other problems. Do not write anything that will give away who wrote it. Give enough information so that the problem can be answered. The leader will collect the folded slips to start Task I.

Task I: A teacher-appointed panel of four members will read one third of the problems out loud to the total group. Each panel member will give a brief piece of advice.

Task II: A leader will read another third of the problems. Each Family will decide on one solution or suggestion to solve the problem. This response will be shared with the Community.

Task III: The remaining problems will be put into a hat and drawn one at a time—each time by a different Community member. This person will give personal opinions and suggestions regarding the problem drawn. Please give illustrations or anecdotes.

> **Thinking About This.** *How do I feel about the solution given for my problem? What about it was good? Not-so-good? Poor? What attitudes were used as the responses were given? Did I express the problem clearly enough? Accurately? Honestly? Which method of answering (panel, Family, individual, etc.) did I find the most interesting? Helpful? Sincere?*
>
> **Sharing (Family).** *Write a problem that you wish to share with your Family. Our Family may use any method we wish to respond honestly and with a loving, caring and sharing attitude. Ask a specific member for special advice or suggestions. Be aware of your own feelings about being open. Share your degree of reluctance on being open and vulnerable.*

BUSINESS

> ***Challenge.*** *A corporation is several people working together. They cooperate to PLAN, ORGANIZE and BE a business.*

Explore

✎ Your Co-worker group is a corporation who will develop the "Survival Kit." This kit will contain your group plans. The kit must fit inside a plastic baggie. The product is to be a "what every person needs in their pocket or locker." Make your own final product name.

A. Your first task is to decide the following roles. Research and write job descriptions. Then, discover a workable method to fill these roles.

President: _____

_____

_____

_____

Advertising/Sales:_____

_____

_____

_____

Vice President:_____

_____

_____

_____

Secretary: _____

_____

_____

_____

Bookkeeper/Treasurer:_____

_____

_____

_____

B. Now, use group brainstorming to gather ideas for what the kit will contain. (Use your Journal to enter ideas also.)

_____   _____
_____   _____
_____   _____
_____   _____
_____   _____
_____   _____

C. How many will be made? (Consider the alloted time frame suggested by the teacher.) Discuss how you decided this.

_____
_____
_____
_____
_____
_____

How do we get the investment capital to do a sampling? _____

_____
_____
_____
_____
_____

D. After a teacher-defined time for sales your task is to analyze your costs/profits.

Number made:_____   Number sold: _____

Cost each: _____   Price each:_____

Total cost:_____   Total income: _____

Total hours spent: _____   Profit: _____

Amount workers made per hour: _____

How much investors made on their investment:_____

✎ My Evaluation

My own role and what I learned about myself: _____

_____
_____

✎ My Co-workers and what I learned about each of them.

NAME	WHAT I LEARNED
1. _____	_____
	_____
2. _____	_____
	_____
3. _____	_____
	_____
4. _____	_____
	_____
5. _____	_____
	_____
6. _____	_____
	_____

✎ Thoughts about improving the product/process:

_____

_____

_____

_____

_____

Thinking About This. I will decide the role I played and the degree of success I had in doing it as I did. I will now decide the role(s) each of my co-workers used and their individual degree of success. Where did each person apply (or misdirect) individual skills and interests? What helpful hints can I give each of them to improve their role in the process of creating and interacting? (I will list these specifically behind each co-worker's name.)

Sharing (Co-Workers). Share your evaluations of your own role in the process of working together with product development and sales. After each of you gives your own evaluation share your gentle, constructive evaluation of the others—how well they did and helpful hints. Some companies will be given a chance to develop a new product and demonstrate the process in front of the Community. (The product will be given to you when you get with the Community.)

I CAN'T MARRY A FRIEND

> **Challenge.** *I counseled a young adult who was about to marry an abusive person. I asked if there wasn't a good, gentle, loving person who would be a better mate. "Oh yes, a very special one—but NOT to marry. That person is my friend! I couldn't marry a friend."*

Explore

✎ Think on the idea of "love." What are six qualities of a good, loving relationship?

1. _____
2. _____
3. _____
4. _____
5. _____
6. _____

✎ What do you already know about love? (Define love.)

_____
_____
_____
_____
_____
_____
_____

✎ What do you need yet to learn? (How can you know what you need?)

_____
_____
_____
_____
_____
_____
_____

✎ Describe a good mate. Incorporate your ideas from above into that person.

_____

_____

_____

_____

_____

_____

_____

_____

_____

_____

_____

_____

_____

_____

_____

_____

Thinking About This. *Who do I know who has the qualities of successful friendship in their marriage or relationship? What do I see that works for them? What doesn't work in a poor relationship? What qualities must I acquire to be a good mate? What are the top five qualities I feel I must have in a friendship/marriage?*

Sharing (Family). *Each member of your Family is going to share their own qualities and those of their "ideal" mate. Assist them in describing the qualities. Gently prod them to give everyday examples of how each quality would exhibit itself in both of the people.*

You are now going to be assigned a Mate (or will remain single). Meet with your mate in the Community setting. Have a Community member present a "relationship" problem. Our task is to role play the successful solution to that problem. Four or five Community members will give feedback to your solution. Be gentle, yet clear and "real!"

WHERE TO LIVE

> ***Challenge.*** *Some people spend less time choosing WHERE they will live than what clothes to wear. It may be wise to consider the geographic location of your "dream house."*

Explore

✎ Pick a definite spot where you might want to live include exact city, neighborhood and street.

_____

_____

_____

_____

✎ Now, consider its location in relation to the following:

Getting to work

_____

_____

_____

_____

Going to school or career training location

_____

_____

_____

_____

Shopping

_____

_____

_____

_____

Convenience to your friends

_____

_____

_____

_____

Distance to your families

_____

_____

_____

_____

Distance to entertainment

_____

_____

_____

_____

✎ Describe the house you want to live in. (Both inside and out.)

_____

_____

_____

_____

✎ What special "spaces" are yours alone? Others? (Be specific.)

_____

_____

_____

_____

_____

**Thinking About This.** What major issues, agreements, disagreements, or differences to these decisions come up in our relationship? How can we resolve them with our mutual loving, caring and sharing? Who gets the last word?

**Sharing (Mate).** How can you both decide on a place to live? (A wife wanted to vacation in New York, the husband in San Franscisco. A compromise is half-way in between—St. Louis. An alternative is a location that they BOTH want!) Pick other challanging topics. Discuss how to arrive at a compromise. At an alternative.

OH OH!

> **Challenge.** *Your life has run into a "significant snag" that will test the mettle of the partnership with your mate.*

Explore

✎ Discuss with your Mate the possible challenges that occur in any good relationship. (Assume mutual loyalty and fidelity in a monogomous, heterosexual relationship.)

_____
_____
_____
_____
_____
_____
_____
_____
_____

✎ Rank order according to the hardest for you to deal with. Discuss these issues and each of you write a workable solution to the two biggest challenges.

Challenge 1 Solution

_____
_____
_____
_____

Challenge 2 Solution

_____
_____
_____
_____
_____

✎ List what probably cannot be settled in these two challenges and why.

Challenge 1 Differences

_____

_____

_____

_____

_____

Challenge 2 Differences

_____

_____

_____

_____

_____

Thinking About This. *How have I seen challenges dealt with successfully by both partners "winning?" What are examples of "no-win" ways to deal with challenges? What is "win-lose?"*

Sharing (Mate). *Discuss each of your important challenges and possible solutions. Did your mates write the same solutions as yours after the discussion? Why? Explain. Share "win-win" examples. "No-win" examples. "Win-lose." Who should win in a partnership? Why? How? Define "alternatives." Give examples. Should couples interact as they do on TV shows such as "Dating Game" and "Newly Weds?" Role play some "win-win" challenges. "Win-lose." Share with the Community.*

WORK NEEDED

> ***Challenge.*** *America has the staggering task of creating an average of 100,000 new jobs every week for the next 10 years to meet the expanding job market. That figure, which represents a total of five million new jobs a year is what will be needed to provide work for three major groups: 1) first-time job seekers, 2) workers who have been displaced by automation and 3) the unemployed.*

Explore

✎ Use your Co-workers group to brainstorm ways to create new jobs. (Remember, YOU are NOW, or soon will be, in the first-time job seekers catagory. Rank order the 10 most workable ideas. Be prepared to support your decisions. Invent or discover jobs if necessary.

1._____
2._____
3._____
4._____
5._____
6._____
7._____
8._____
9._____
10._____

> ***Thinking About This.*** *I will assume the responsibility for developing one of these five ideas into a presentation to my Co-worker group and then the Community.*
>
> ***Sharing (Co-workers).*** *Refine your ideas into a short report. Combine your report with others in the Community to create a formal presentation. Send copies to top officials in our state and Washington, D.C.*

© 1992, JIST Works, Inc. • Indianapolis, Indiana

LIFESTYLES

> ***Challenge.*** *Cowboys are seen as enjoying the outdoors and living a rough and rustic life in the saddle and around campfires. They rarely complain. Pioneers are seen as traveling across the country and settling the land. They are hearty souls living in covered wagons.*

Explore

✎ Your task is to characterize other lifestyles. Explain what you "know" about each of the following types of people. (Use your Journal for extra writing paper). Describe their personal life, social activities, families, early and later goals in life and levels of fun, enjoyment, satisfaction, love and growth.

The Monetarily Affluent

_____

_____

_____

_____

Protestors

_____

_____

_____

_____

Politicians

_____

_____

_____

_____

Preachers

_____

_____

_____

_____

Financially Destitute

_____

_____

_____

_____

Teachers

_____

_____

_____

_____

Thinking About This. *What other lifestyle types do I know? I will find one of these people in my neighborhood to interview. I will prepare the interview questions and review them with my Family before I actually visit.*

Sharing (Family). *Share the results of the interviews with your Family and then with the Community. Discuss other lifestyle types and what they do in all phases of their lives.*

SIMULATION II—A MAJOR CHALLENGE

You and your Mate have been faced with a major life CHALLENGE. (Pick from your high priority list in OH OH! or have your leader/instructor give you a situation to handle.) You must work together to:

1. Focus on the problem.
2. Think of options.
3. Get information on the options/solutions.
4. Discuss a way of cooperative decision making.
5. Make a plan.
6. Carry out the plan—keeping options open for alternative solutions.

You will use the "real" community facilities—counselors, psychologists, social workers, friends, family, etc.

✎ Document the problem and the problem-solving methods as shown above (or an alternate one that is more workable for you). You will be sharing your complete process from picking the challenging problem to the solutions and the options.

The major challenge (describe in detail).

_____

_____

_____

_____

How does the problem affect you and your Mate? (Be specific.)

_____

_____

_____

_____

✎ What are your first steps toward a solution?

1._____ 5._____

2._____ 6._____

3._____ 7._____

4._____ 8._____

✎ Where can you get information?

_____

_____

_____

_____

✎ What is the solution you would like to see happen?

_____

_____

_____

_____

✎ List five specific ways you can work together toward a solution.

1. _____
2. _____
3. _____
4. _____
5. _____

✎ What problems do you anticipate?

_____

_____

_____

_____

✎ What are your next steps toward a solution?

_____

_____

_____

_____

✎ How can you keep your options open for alternate solutions?

_____

_____

_____

_____

SELF-INVENTORY II

> **Challenge.** *I will evaluate myself. How am I doing so far? Before I begin answering this question, I will review my responses in Section II and what I have learned about myself.*

Explore

✎ Ask yourself these questions honestly and with a fair degree of self-examination.

CHARACTERISTIC	CIRCLE ONE		
	LOW		HIGH
My Level of Sincerity			
Desire to do my best	1	2	3
Attempt to learn more	1	2	3
Wish to cooperate	1	2	3
My Research			
Use of many sources	1	2	3
Clear, straight-forward responses	1	2	3
Attempt to find more resources	1	2	3
My Awareness of Self			
Discovering new things......................	1	2	3
Desire to improve	1	2	3
Working on personal challenges	1	2	3
My Awareness of Others			
Cooperation in groups......................	1	2	3
Level of ability to communicate ideas	1	2	3
Ability to assist others	1	2	3
My Written and Oral Products			
Quality of oral reports	1	2	3
Excellence of written work...................	1	2	3
Amount of preparation for work	1	2	3
The Carry-Over Outside School			
Homework................................	1	2	3
Degree of interest in my studies	1	2	3
Hobbies and interests that relate	1	2	3
Overall Sense of Personal Satisfaction			
My satisfaction in my personal growth	1	2	3
Ability to increase my friendships............	1	2	3
Amount of available energy used..............	1	2	3
Degree progressed toward my potential	1	2	3

FAMILY INVENTORY II

Challenge. *I will evaluate my Family honestly and lovingly.*

Explore

✎ Now that you have completed the second Simulation in this book, express your opinions about your Family. Again, think carefully how your Family worked together.

CHARACTERISTIC	CIRCLE ONE		
	LOW		HIGH
Level Of Sincerity			
Our desire to do our best	1	2	3
Our attempt to learn more	1	2	3
Comments: _____			
Research			
Use of many sources	1	2	3
Clear, straight-forward sharing	1	2	3
Comments: _____			
Awareness			
Our attempt to listen to other's ideas	1	2	3
Effectiveness of Family communication	1	2	3
Comments: _____			
Cooperation			
Level at which we worked together	1	2	3
Our understanding of other's needs	1	2	3
Comments: _____			
Products			
Completion of our work	1	2	3
Clarity of our work	1	2	3
Appearance of our work	1	2	3
Comments: _____			

✎ I will use this format to make entries into my Journal to evaluate and make suggestions to my Friends, Co-workers, and the Community. We will share these evaluations among our groups.

MOVING ON

I have discovered more about myself in Section II. I have explored the depth of my relationships with Family, Friends and Co-workers, and discovered a new part of me that exists for my life partner.

In Section III we will examine levels of involvement, caring for others, service projects, work, lifestyles, global challenges and world concerns. But more challenges await.

Perhaps you will be faced with financial problems or raising a child by yourself or with your mate. You have been successful so far because you know you can succeed. You will find that same attitude of success in Section III.

Remember

- ✎ *You are already successful because your attitude is one of accepting present success.*
- ✎ *You are a loving, caring and sharing person—and it shows.*
- ✎ *You find satisfaction in interacting successfully with others.*
- ✎ *You can manage your own life and at the same time, assist others.*
- ✎ *The world needs you—you have the solutions to its challenges.*

The World Around Us

In Section I and II you have had many experiences in managing life. You have a Family that is loving, caring and sharing. You have explored the vast world of schooling and training. You have Friends with whom you have shared opinions, job options and life challenges. And you have a Community that is supportive and caring.

You have traveled a short time with a Mate—sharing dreams, aspirations, fears and joys. You have had fun, enjoyment, satisfaction, love and growth and have begun to plan a future together exploring its challenges.

You are about to have further adventures. You could have an attitude of "Wow! Am I ready for this?" Or, you could feel, "Wow! I AM ready for any challenge."

As you venture into new territory of personal and social growth you will be interacting with a world that needs healing. Your inner thought could be, "Please give me strength, wisdom and love!"

YOU ARE IN CONTROL

> **Challenge.** *You have control over just TWO things in your interaction with others (and with situations)—your DISTANCE (geograpical or emotional) and the amount of ENERGY that you put into the relationship or situation.*

Explore

✎ In the following situations you will decide: 1) The distance (how close or how far), and 2) How much energy you will invest in a situation such as this. Circle the numbers that fit and briefly explain why. Add three situations of your own.

THE SITUATION	DISTANCE CLOSE/FAR			ENERGY MUCH/NONE		
A boss scolds you unfairly. Others overhear.	1	2	3	1	2	3
A boss scolds you fairly. Others overhear.	1	2	3	1	2	3
A friend asks for comfort for a family death.	1	2	3	1	2	3
Your child screams, "I wanted French fries!"	1	2	3	1	2	3
Your parent(s) keeps you from your date.	1	2	3	1	2	3
Your date breaks your "date" as others listen.	1	2	3	1	2	3
A friend offers you an illegal substance.	1	2	3	1	2	3
A teacher suggests that you have cheated.	1	2	3	1	2	3
A vicious rumor starts about you.	1	2	3	1	2	3
You discover that you have a serious illness.	1	2	3	1	2	3
A friend wants to marry you.	1	2	3	1	2	3
(Your Own)	1	2	3	1	2	3
(Your Own)	1	2	3	1	2	3
(Your Own)	1	2	3	1	2	3

✎ Think of three people in your life. Do not use their names, but describe their relationship to you using metaphors. (What is a metaphor?)

Example #1: *"My friend is a butterfly who lights gently, shares beauty briefly, then flutters away to share with others."*

Example #2: *"An acquaintance is a bull dozer who roars into my life, breaks up my peace of mind and shoves the pieces into a messy pile."*

Person #1: _____

_____

_____

_____

Person #2: _____

_____

_____

_____

Person #3: _____

_____

_____

_____

Thinking About This. *Who, in my life, demands the most energy yet wants the most distance? How does this make me feel? What can I do? Who wants to be close yet gives little energy? What about my feelings? My thoughts? Who do I want to be close and share my energy? How can I do that without pushing them away? What is the "dance?"*

Sharing (Family). *Discuss each situation and your comments. Is it OK to vary distances and energies with different people? Explain the distances and energies invested or demanded. What happens if someone is demanding much closeness and high energy and we only desire low energy and much distance? Do a skit or role play to show ways to handle a situation such as this.*

SERVICE PROJECTS

> ***Challenge.*** *One of the privileges you have in life is to share your personal self with others. You have been discovering your special interests and abilities. Some of these can be shared with others. Imagine yourself giving your time and abilities to others.*

Explore

✎ Who in your neighborhood, school or workplace would appreciate having you give of your time and abilities?

1. _____
2. _____
3. _____
4. _____
5. _____
6. _____

✎ How much time a week would you give?

✎ What would you share with these people? (List five of your "gifts.")

1. _____
2. _____
3. _____
4. _____
5. _____

✎ Here are some things to consider when giving of your personal self.

How will you go to these people?

_____
_____
_____

What are convenient times? For you? For them?

_____
_____
_____

What are some things to take?

_____

_____

_____

What are some possible problems? What are their solutions?

_____

_____

_____

Who will you go with?

_____

_____

_____

What are other considerations?

_____

_____

_____

✎ Did you have trouble thinking of ideas? Perhaps these suggestions will help.

  • If you want to give of yourself to children participate in their arts, crafts, plays, music, games, collections, food, toys, etc.

  • If you want to give of yourself to adults and senior citizens consider reading books, bringing gifts, conversation, yard work, carpentry, socializing, crafts, food services, providing transportation, etc.

✎ Plan your project (what to do, share or provide).

_____

_____

_____

✎ When can you start?

_____

✎ Who is the contact person(s)?

_____

Thinking About This. *Complete this section after your project.*

✎ How do I know they appreciated my service?

_____

_____

_____

✎ How do I feel about what I did?

_____

_____

_____

✎ How would I do it differently next time?

_____

_____

_____

✎ When will I do it next?

_____

_____

_____

✎ What will I do?

_____

_____

_____

Sharing (Family). *Share your thoughts and feelings. Tell of your experiences in planning and carrying out your project. Make your own questions to ask each other about this project. Share your activities with the community in a unique way.*

BUT, WHAT DOES IT MEAN TO ME?

> ***Challenge.*** *I was applying for my first job after college as a vocational rehabilitation counselor. In the interview, trying to impress the director with my concern for others, I blurted out, "I have an 'apathy' for people." He said nothing but looked amused.*
>
> *After being hired, the director called me aside, and with a humorous tone said, "By the way, the word you meant to say was 'EMPATHY'."*

Explore

✎ What is empathy? Give an example from your life.

_____

_____

_____

_____

✎ Define and illustrate apathy.

_____

_____

_____

_____

✎ List six words besides empathy that describe a positive caring for others.

1. _____   4. _____

2. _____   5. _____

3. _____   6. _____

✎ List six words that define a negative attitude toward others.

1. _____   4. _____

2. _____   5. _____

3. _____   6. _____

✎ List four words you could use to show a postive attitude toward yourself. Think of situations when you project that attitude.

WORD	THE SITUATION
1.	
2.	
3.	
4.	

✎ You may also display a negative response to your thoughts or actions. Describe three of them.

WORD	THE SITUATION
1.	
2.	
3.	

Thinking About This. *When is it easy to have empathy? Hard? With whom? Why? Am I a "feeling" person? How do I know? Explain. Discuss "apathy" in the world today. Is there apathy in my life? What can I do to change the situation?*

Sharing (Family). *Discuss empathy, apathy, words that hurt, words that heal and words that cause ill feelings. Give examples in each. Do some people get hurt even if you attempt to be healing or loving? Who? Why? When? What should be your reaction? Response? Role play some empathy, apathy, and healing situations.*

PERSPECTIVE

> ***Challenge.*** *I will look at those around me and also inside myself. What did I bring with me into this life? What will I take out? What of me will I leave behind?*

Explore

✎ Write about two accomplishments in your life.

1._____

_____

_____

2._____

_____

_____

✎ Now share two personal satisfactions (i.e., ways you have made other person's lives better through planning and carrying it out).

1._____

_____

_____

2._____

_____

_____

✎ Notice that you have been brought closer to several people during this program. Describe the closeness you feel with the following:

Family Members

_____

_____

_____

Friends

_____

_____

_____

Co-workers

_____

_____

_____

A Mate

_____

_____

_____

✎ You have a better idea now what you want to give and what you expect from each of the person's mentioned above. Use this space to jot down some words or short phrases that will remind you what to share with your Mate/Friends when you have your discussion. Be as honest, open and willing as you care to at this time.

KEY WORDS / THOUGHTS	
_____	_____
_____	_____
_____	_____
_____	_____
_____	_____
_____	_____
_____	_____

Thinking About This. *I will be happy about my accomplishments no matter how large or small. How do I feel when I accomplish something I've set out to do? Why? When have I not accomplished what I wanted to? Why?*

Sharing (Mate/Friends). *Share our accomplishments, satisfactions and closeness with our "significant others." Discuss what you should expect in life regarding closeness, satisfactions and accomplishments. What is expecting too much? Too little? What are the best ways to get these? Worst ways?*

COMMUNITY

> ***Challenge.*** *The concept of a community with sharing of goods, services and responsibiliites is as old as Homo sapiens. "Common-ism" is the basis of all sharing. It doesn't work when selfishness becomes a major factor.*

Explore

✎ Write definitions for each of the terms below.

Community

_____

_____

_____

Sharing

_____

_____

_____

Commonwealth

_____

_____

_____

Voting

_____

_____

_____

Concensus

_____

_____

_____

Majority

_____

_____

_____

Constitution

_____

_____

_____

> ***Thinking About This.*** *How has the original concept of communal sharing been modified by political systems? What is capitalism? Where are these systems used? How are they changing? How is my own financial system at home set up? How would I change it?*
>
> ***Sharing (Co-workers).*** *Discuss the terms and how each relate to how you are experiencing the world. How can you make it better? Where do you feel helpless? What is "communalism?" Is it workable? Devise a short skit to present a view of sharing or selfishness. Present it to the community.*

✎ Your Ideas for the Skit:

THOUGHTS	HOW TO PRESENT THE THOUGHT
1. _____	_____
_____	_____
2. _____	_____
_____	_____
3. _____	_____
_____	_____
4. _____	_____
_____	_____

FADS AND FOLKWAYS

Challenge. *Not everybody does things the way I do. In my neighborhood are hundreds of different ways people dress, think, act or interact.*

Explore

✎ Research the following terms. Provide definitions (in your own words) and give examples from your life.

Fads

_____

_____

_____

_____

_____

Folkways

_____

_____

_____

Mores

_____

_____

_____

Colloquialisms

_____

_____

_____

Slang

_____

_____

_____

✎ What is YOUR opinion of the way things are going NOW? Be definite! Be specific! Take a stand, but be wise. Do this in a way that you make an impact on others. It can be written, then read or an impromptu monolog. You will share it with your Community. Find others who feel the same — get them to co-present with you in a powerful way.

_____

_____

_____

_____

_____

_____

_____

✎ Questions to ask yourself (and those presenting with you) might be as follows. Do I (we) have to be aggressive? What is another way? What is my (our) best method of presentation? What do we need? What is my (our) specific point? What is my (our) objective? What am I (we) attempting to change? Solidify? Emphasize? What is my (our) strengths in changing the world? Changing others? Changing ourselves? Our weaknesses? Use this space to begin your planning.

_____

_____

_____

_____

_____

_____

_____

_____

> ***Thinking About This.*** *I will imagine that I now live 100 years into the future. I will describe a typical day (using examples from the above concepts.) What is my role in joining in or changing the world? Others? Myself?*
>
> ***Sharing (Friends).*** *Share your working definitions of the concepts, examples from your life and your 21st century day. Share some of these with the Community. Get specific now! Give YOUR opinion how things are going now!*

I CAN 'T

Explore

✎ Take each of these words and tell why they are NOT workable words—how they lead to negative thinking. Give an example of each in your life.

Try · Fail · Can't · Attempt · Dumb · Lazy · Useless

Try

_____
_____
_____

Fail

_____
_____
_____

Can't

_____
_____
_____

Attempt

_____
_____
_____

Dumb

_____
_____
_____

Lazy

_____

_____

_____

Useless

_____

_____

_____

✎ What other words are not workable? (Turn you off, aggravate or disgust you, etc.) Tell why, when, how and who uses it.

WORD	WHY, WHEN, HOW, AND WHO USES IT?
1. _____	_____
_____	_____
2. _____	_____
_____	_____
3. _____	_____
_____	_____
4. _____	_____
_____	_____
5. _____	_____
_____	_____

Thinking About This. *Should I strike these words from my vocabulary? Do they serve a purpose? What is a workable word? What are antonyms for each?*

Sharing (Family). *Why are "try" and "attempt" used so often yet each implies the possibility of failure? Give examples of people who asked you to try or attempt, yet you sensed they knew you would not do as "well" as they required. Tell your stories and give better words that encourage growth and facilitate the ability to make decisions.*

© 1992, JIST Works, Inc. • Indianapolis, Indiana

SYSTEMS RESTRUCTURED

> **Challenge.** *Planet XYZ in the Andromeda Galaxy is a world with no boundaries, having learned to become "world" citizens rather than citizens of a country. They live in peace and harmony without conflict and war. They have refined their internal social structures to a point of enjoying smooth operating systems.*

Explore

✎ Use this concept to discuss briefly the ways each of the following is a system. Give an example of each.

Ecology (Eco-system)

_____

_____

_____

Politics (Political Systems)

_____

_____

_____

Food (Food Systems)

_____

_____

_____

Money (Monetary Systems)

_____

_____

_____

Spiritual (Religious Systems)

_____

_____

_____

Learning (Educational Systems)

_____

_____

_____

✎ What other systems are there? Make some up. Tell what they do and how they work.

System #1: _____

_____

_____

_____

System #2: _____

_____

_____

_____

System #3: _____

_____

_____

_____

System #4: _____

_____

_____

_____

Thinking About This. *I will visualize our planet Earth as having no borders. I will then visualize and describe the "systems" working perfectly within the Spaceship Earth concept.*

Sharing (Co-workers). *Design an instructional unit about an Interactive System. Do not duplicate the system of any other group in your class. Discuss how you can do that. Demonstrate how your systems can be built into a world-wide system.*

GLOBAL CHALLENGE

> **Challenge.** *The President's Global 2000 Report warns that if present trends continue, the world in 2000 will be more crowded, more polluted, less stable ecologically, and more vulnerable to disruption than the world we now live in.*
>
> *The report concludes that only sound, managed resource development could help create a better life.*

Explore

✎ We are the generation of tomorrow. We have inherited our freedom to ignore or be challenged by puzzlings problems. Being conscious of the situation is the first step toward solving the problems. The ideas that you generate could well be the next step to enriching the world.

PROBLEM	IDEAS TO SOLVE EACH PROBLEM
world food shortage	
overfished and exploited lakes, rivers and oceans	
air pollution and climate warming gasses	
soil depletion and deforestation	

PROBLEM	IDEAS TO SOLVE EACH PROBLEM
acid rain and destruction of ozone layer	
overcrowded living conditions	
overpopulation	

Thinking About This. This is OUR world! I am an adult with family and community responsibilities. What can I do about this mess? What will my personal and family life be like in the year 2000 if we (including me) do not do something about these situations right away? How am I contributing to the problem? To the solution? I will write my first thoughts (personal brainstorm) about my plans for saving this planet and making life better (and more loving). Do these global problems unite us? How does working together to tackle these challenges make me a better person? What can I do NOW?

Sharing (Family). Discuss your individual plans. Prepare a Family statement that reflects the plans and commitments of each member. Share this with the Community. Submit copies to the appropriate persons in government, business, industry, etc. Press THEM for a response and a commitment.

GO TO THE TOP!

> ***Challenge.*** *Sometimes it is necessary to go to the top to get what you NEED or WANT DONE. This may mean writing to the President of the United States or chief executive officer of a large corporation. Somehow get to the person you want.*

Explore

✎ You are interested in making the world a better place to live. You must first know more in your specific area of interest. Pick an area of personal concern.

Some Possible Topics

- Sea Life
- Endangered Species
- Conservation Techniques
- Medicines

- World Food Sources
- Monetary Systems
- Other_____
- Other_____

✎ Do some research on your topic of concern. Where can you get more information on your topic? Organize your sources of research in the area below. Examples of possible sources: phonebook, community resource books, local, state or federal agencies, Department of Agriculture, NASA, senators and congress, representatives, Department of Education, County Agricultural Extension Agencies, Health Department, U.S. Information Office (Pueblo, Colorado), Office of the President, Forestry Department, etc. Contact sources of information (postcard, toll free telephone, etc.) to ask for free information.

Sources of Information / Addresses / What I want to know

_____

_____

_____

_____

_____

_____

_____

_____

✎ You have explored. Now, get something done! Start with your objective and devise a plan to get something done.

Your objective

_____

_____

_____

_____

Your plan

_____

_____

_____

_____

Who is working with you?

_____

_____

_____

_____

How you can work together?

_____

_____

_____

_____

What else?

_____

_____

_____

_____

Thinking About This. *Who else has my same concern? How can I get together with them? What would we do? First, I should ... then ...*

Sharing (Family). *Report your concern(s), information and possible solutions to the Community. What now? How will you know you got what you want? How do you get from here to there?*

PUBLIC SERVICE ANNOUNCEMENT

> **Challenge.** *Our lives are influenced daily by the written and spoken word. We are informed, teased and goaded into action by the media. The freedom of speech guarantees our right to act based on the knowledge that we have.*

Explore

✎ Name a written and spoken word, both public and private, that has most influenced you. How? (Be specific.)

WORD	WRITTEN	SPOKEN
PUBLIC		
PRIVATE		

✎ Write short public announcements, ads and "fillers" that present your point of view regarding your personal life, your community and/or planetary concern. Work alone or with others with a similiar concern.

My two biggest areas of interest and concern:

1. _____

_____

_____

2. _____

_____

_____

_____

Ideas for presentation

1. _____

_____

2. _____

_____

3. _____

_____

4. _____

_____

5. _____

_____

6. _____

_____

7. _____

_____

8. _____

_____

9. _____

_____

10. _____

_____

> ***Thinking About This.*** *How can I get my concerns made public? Does the media help or hinder the efforts of concerned citizens with a cause? Who controls the media? Who influences the media? Can I influence the media?*
>
> ***Sharing (Family/Co-workers/Community).*** *Try out your presentation. Be open to new ideas, revisions, suggestions. Write! Revise! Write! Revise! Then, make your actual contacts and presentations to the Community. Decide your plan for exposure to the general public (from church announcements to newspaper, radio and TV).*

WAVE OF THE FUTURE

> ***Challenge.*** *The president of France sponsored a meeting of the top writers, artists and other creators. They were to discover ways to tie cultural activities into the economic system. They reasoned that the present economy is based on the soon-to-be-outdated economy of autos, steel and hardware.*
>
> *The new wave is micro-technology — a computer-based science information storage and retrieval system. The conference emphasized the need to tie the old and traditional to the new technology so it will be an integral part of society. The alternative is to lose the traditional cultural values to displays created by microchips.*

Explore

✎ Very soon in your life your talents and products are going to be used in a high technology, computer-based world. Your task is to keep the electronic age from de-humanizing people. Your energy must be used to nurture the "eternal" values of warmth and caring interaction. Create a plan to use your strengths and interests as valuable tools to make the world a better place. Brainstorm ways to use your abilities and aptitudes in a computer-based world.

_____   _____

_____   _____

_____   _____

_____   _____

_____   _____

_____   _____

> ***Thinking About This.*** *I will write a statement of commitment telling how I will use my specific talents to improve the world. I will include what I think is valuable, beautiful and worth keeping of the traditional. I will give my ideas for changes that are needed. How has the world kept these human values to this point in time? How have I assisted? What professions ensure the keeping of human values? What organizations and institutions?*
>
> ***Sharing (Co-workers).*** *Tell of your personal commitments to use your talents to serve the world—keeping the traditional but stretching your visions of the future. Make a presentation of your ideas to the Community.*

A DAY WITH A POOR FAMILY

> **Challenge.** *"Blessed are the poor in spirit ..." "You will always have the poor with you..." "Share with the poor and you will be rich in spirit."*

Explore

✎ Describe "poor" as both a positive state and an undesirable condition.

As a positive state: _____

_____

_____

_____

As an undesirable condition: _____

_____

_____

_____

✎ Many words have been used to describe poor—financially deprived, economically distressed, disadvantaged, poverty stricken, broke, destitute, out-of-work, etc. Think of some other terms to describe poor.

_____   _____

_____   _____

_____   _____

_____   _____

_____   _____

> **Thinking About This.** *I will imagine being in the condition of "broke" for an extended period of time. I will describe a typical day.*
>
> **Sharing (Family).** *Share your stories in a day of being poor. How are the stories the same? How do they differ? Create skits of things "poor" people do in their time alone and in interaction with others. How do these activities differ from the "rich?" Is poor bad? Good? Explain.*

TIME TRAVEL

> ***Challenge.*** *You are to travel to a different time. Imagine that you see and hear many new people and things. Relax, take a deep breath. Allow your eyes to close half-way. Your thoughts will take you to a different time—backward or forward in time. You can come back to your seat anytime you wish. Remember all the things you see and do in this other time and place. Begin now to close your eyes and off you go ... off ... you ... go ... off ... off ... off into time ... into ... space ... backward or forward ... in ... time ... in ... space ... drifting ...*

Explore

✎ Who are the people you see? Describe their looks. Their surroundings.

_____

_____

_____

_____

✎ How are these people the same as you?

_____

_____

_____

_____

✎ How are they different? What do they do for work?

_____

_____

_____

_____

✎ Play?

_____

_____

_____

_____

✎ Social activities?

_____

_____

_____

_____

✎ Spiritual activities?

_____

_____

_____

_____

✎ What problems do they have?

_____

_____

_____

_____

✎ What solutions do they have?

_____

_____

_____

_____

> ***Thinking About This.*** *Did I go backward or forward in time? Why? Did I like it better there? Why? Would I like to live there or just visit? Did I learn anything that would make my world better?*
>
> ***Sharing (Family).*** *Share aspects about your trips and the people (in detail). If you had trouble visualizing, just IMAGINE that you "saw." Pretend!*

A NEW WORLD

> ***Challenge.*** *"This century should be remembered as the time when science uncovered the mysteries of the universe and people were recognized as having controlled their natural impulses to destroy."*
> —***Dr. Victor Weisskops***, *Physicist*

Explore

✎ Brainstorm ways YOU (personally) control impulses that potentially harm or destroy.

_____   _____

_____   _____

_____   _____

_____   _____

_____   _____

✎ What do you think and feel is the present condition of the world?

_____

_____

_____

_____

✎ What will happen if aggression continues?

_____

_____

_____

_____

✎ Define LOVE and how it can be used in your world.

_____

_____

_____

_____

✎ Describe a plan for extending LOVE into the world you experience. Be specific!

_____

_____

_____

_____

✎ What are three ways you are able to cope with the aggression of others.

1. _____

_____

_____

2. _____

_____

_____

3. _____

_____

_____

✎ List two ways that you have seen LOVE "defuse" aggression.

1. _____

_____

_____

2. _____

_____

_____

Thinking About This. *What is my personal role in the making of the future? Be specific regarding aggression (mine and others) and love (mine and others).*

Sharing (Mate/Friends). *Discuss how you see the state of the world. How you see your own personal life. Create a joint plan to make the world a better place for you, your family, your child(ren) and others. Share this with the Community. Demonstrate love and aggression to the Family and the Community.*

DISCOVERY

Explore

✎ Relax for a few minutes. Think of five discoveries that need to be made to help the world. Be specific.

1. _____
   _____

2. _____
   _____

3. _____
   _____

4. _____
   _____

5. _____
   _____

Thinking About This. I will pick one discovery that interests me. I'll get into a mood where my thoughts flow fast and freely, writing my ideas describing the discovery that will help the world. I'll be specific and not judge or criticize my flow of ideas. Now, I'll do this with one or two of the other "needed" discoveries.

Sharing (Co-workers). Share your ideas. Pick one of your discoveries to present to the Co-Worker group. Get into the mood where all members add to your ideas about that discovery. Remember, no idea gets evaluated during brainstorming—just jot it down with the other ideas. Share some of your ideas with the Community.

WE ALL AGREE

> **Challenge.** *A concensus occurs when most or all persons have the same opinion or come to an agreement on any one topic. For example: My friends agree that my tuna soufflé is the best that they have ever eaten.*

Explore

✎ What are three specific opinions you have that you think your Mate should have?

1. _____
   _____

2. _____
   _____

3. _____
   _____

✎ List three methods you could use to get your Mate to come to a consensus.

1. _____
   _____

2. _____
   _____

3. _____
   _____

✎ Give three examples when a Family consensus would be important.

1. _____
   _____

2. _____
   _____

3. _____
   _____

✎ What are three other ways for any group to come to an agreement?

1._____

_____

2._____

_____

3._____

_____

✎ What opinions (issues) are the hardest to get everyone to agree on? Why?

1._____

_____

2._____

_____

3._____

_____

✎ Name two things you feel so strongly about that you will probably never change your mind. Be defininte!

1._____

_____

2._____

_____

Thinking About This. *Am I opinionated? Too much? Too little? Where does that help me? Hinder me? What do I do when I conflict with an opinionated person? A Mate? A boss? A Family member? A fellow student?*

Sharing (Family/Mate). *Discuss each of your responses (and reactions) and eventually share your best ones with the Community in a way comfortable to you and helpful to them.*

GO IN STYLE

> **Challenge.** *Your Family is going to spend a week with the family of the president of the United States.*

Explore

✎ The president's social secretary gives you a list of concepts you should know. Work with your Family members to research the terms on the list. Rehearse these among yourselves until all of you are familiar with them.

• formal	• bountiful	• soup du jour	• luncheon
• informal	• cuisine	• appetizer	• corsages
• casual	• banquet	• gourmet	• host(ess)
• high tea	• antipasto	• grace	• protocol
• brunch	• ambrosia	• dessert	• introductions
• ballet	• buffet	• etiquette	• amenities
• symphony	• debutante	• celebrity	• valets
• cultural	• deluxe	• receptions	• waistcoats
• elegant	• entree	• bowing	• MC
• R.S.V.P.	• menu	• procession	• Mr., Mrs., Ms.
• receiving lines	• tipping	• hors d'oeuvres	• courtesy
• seating	• ushers	• a la Carte	• delicatessen
• punctuality	• toasts	• curtsy	• calling cards

✎ What other terms or concepts may be necessary to know?

_____   _____

_____   _____

_____   _____

> **Thinking About This.** *I will write a newspaper article (or a formal letter) telling of my week with the president.*
>
> **Sharing (Family/Community).** *Create some ficticious humorous stories that occured because of your lack of knowledge in some of the "proper" ways to behave with the "elite."*

 © 1992, JIST Works, Inc. • Indianapolis, Indiana

THRIVE, NOT SURVIVE

> **Challenge.** *Experts could compile a list of things to keep you interested in your work. For example: 1) Sit on tacks on boring days to keep from falling asleep, 2) Volunteer to do busy work, and 3) Be a clown to keep others entertained. But, you have better ideas to share.*

Explore

✎ Your task is to brainstorm a list of ways to get the most out of your schooling and training. Make each idea interesting, challenging and socially rewarding.

_____   _____
_____   _____
_____   _____
_____   _____
_____   _____
_____   _____
_____   _____
_____   _____

✎ Write about three of these ideas you can begin doing now. Explain fully.

1. _____
_____
_____
_____

2. _____
_____
_____
_____

3. _____
_____
_____
_____

✎ Brainstorm 10 ways that people, places, things and events get in your way to keep you from your potential. (Pretend to give them power they don't really have unless you give it.)

1._____   6. _____
2._____   7. _____
3._____   8. _____
4._____   9. _____
5._____   10. _____

✎ Describe the power that you give others that they do not deserve.

_____

_____

_____

_____

_____

_____

Thinking About This. Why haven't I done this before? (Or when have I?) What is stopping me? If I must be in school how can I make it more satisfying? Can I do it now? How? What is frightening about that? How can we do it as a group?

Sharing (Family). Discuss your responses from Explore and Thinking About This. What more can you do? When? Why? How? Actually DO some of these things for a few days and discuss the results. (After a few days:) Do things look any different? How? Why? Where? Could your community help you have a more satisfying day in school? Discuss this fully. Cheriot sheep thrive on the poor, rocky soil of Scotland. Why? What does this have to do with making school a better place to be?

AND FREEDOM FOR ALL

> **Challenge.** *"We, the People of the United States, in Order to form a more perfect Union, establish Justice, ensure Domestic Tranquility, Provide for the Common Defense, Promote the General Welfare, and Secure the Blessings of Liberty to Ourselves and our Posterity, do Ordain and Establish the Constitution for the United States of America."*
> **—Preamble to the United States Constitution**

Explore

✎ Rewrite the Preamble in your own words. Practice on separate paper.

_____

_____

_____

_____

_____

_____

_____

_____

✎ Give examples of everyday freedoms we sometimes take for granted.

1. _____

   _____

2. _____

   _____

3. _____

   _____

4. _____

   _____

5. _____

   _____

✎ List five ways people's freedoms are being violated today.

1. _____
_____

2. _____
_____

3. _____
_____

4. _____
_____

5. _____
_____

✎ Which violation you listed REALLY bothers YOU and interferes with your personal life? Tell how and what you can do to regain personal power.

_____
_____
_____
_____
_____
_____
_____
_____
_____

Thinking About This. Why are people's freedoms being violated in the world today? In what way? By whom? For what purpose? Where are my own freedoms violated or in jepardy? By whom? Why? Who is benefitting? What can I do about it? Should I? What is my plan?

Sharing (Family/Mate). Work with your Family to discuss one of your plans to attain the goal of a personal sense of freedom in a specific area of your life. Combine your plan with another member of the group with a similiar sense of restriction and a sensible plan for freedom. Share with the Community.

RIGHTS, DUTIES, LEVELS OF INVOLVEMENT

Challenge. *A young woman was attacked and murdered in a Queens, N.Y. housing project. Her screams were heard around the entire project—but no one would get involved enough to even call the police. Although many saw the incident, no one did a thing about it.*

Explore

✎ Why didn't people respond to this woman's need?

_____

_____

_____

_____

✎ What would YOU have done?

_____

_____

_____

_____

✎ Describe what you think should be the IDEAL level of involvement between each of the following persons.

A young married couple

_____

_____

_____

_____

Two close friends

_____

_____

_____

_____

A boss with an employee

_____

_____

_____

_____

A citizen with his/her country

_____

_____

_____

_____

Co-workers with each other

_____

_____

_____

_____

A person with the world's problems

_____

_____

_____

_____

A parent with children

_____

_____

_____

_____

✎ Think of seven situations of your own and give the ideal levels of involvement.

1. _____

_____

_____

_____

2. _____

_____

_____

_____

3. _____

_____

_____

_____

4. _____

_____

_____

_____

5. _____

_____

_____

_____

6. _____

_____

_____

_____

7. _____

_____

_____

_____

Thinking About This. *Can a person be TOO involved? How? When? Why? Could I be involved in too many causes? What ones SHOULD I be involved in— without a doubt? What one should I, personally, avoid? Why? How? Where am I indifferent? (What does that really mean?)*

Sharing (Family/Mate). *Discuss your responses and reactions to the above topics. How involved do you want the other Family members in your life to be? Do our walls go up and down at different times to decide how much to let others into our individual lives? How close should Mates be?*

NETWORKING

One example of a network would be a video game enthusiast with a home game computer using a modem to play with others, then going to district competitions (with all the people and things there). The outer ripple may be national or international competitions.

Explore

✎ Research the concept of "network." Give examples of three networks that have YOU as the center. Describe the people, ideas, objects and systems in each of your circles—inner to outer. Use scrap paper. Put the finished written product in the space provided here.

1. _____

_____

_____

2. _____

_____

_____

3. _____

_____

_____

Thinking About This. *What networks am I involved in? To what degree? What other networks interest me? How can I become a part of one of them? What is my plan? What is my level of commitment to join in the network?*

Sharing (Family/Mate). *Do families function better when most members are part of the same network? How much should the lives of family members intermingle? Do similar personalities attract? Repel? Who should give up interests in a partner situation to please the other? Alternatives? Compromise. Share with the Community.*

OIL GLUTTONS

> **Challenge.** *Imagine a world with no oil or other products made from oil.*

Explore

✎ Work with your co-workers. Brainstorm 10 oil-based products that are very important to your life.

1._____   6._____
2._____   7._____
3._____   8._____
4._____   9._____
5._____   10._____

✎ Brainstorm 10 ways your life would be different without oil products.

1._____   6._____
2._____   7._____
3._____   8._____
4._____   9._____
5._____   10._____

✎ Create a plan to thrive in an oil-free world.

_____
_____
_____
_____
_____

> **Thinking About This.** *I will write what I expect a day to be like in a world without oil (transportation, food gathering, necessities, luxuries, social, etc.).*
>
> **Sharing (Co-workers).** *Discuss your ideas of a world without oil dependence. What are the consequences of oil dependence? Tell the Community of your ideas. How would our level of commitment to conservation and cut-backs affect our standard of living?*

ON YOUR OWN

Challenge. *My daughter looked me straight in the eye. "I know I can now make it on my own!" she said, almost defiantly. A thrill went up my spine. She was asserting confidence in her own abilities. We had both feared and looked forward to this day. My daughter was now a woman.*

"All right," I said, "Let's work out a plan that we can both agree on. Decide where you want your own place to live, a way to make your own money and a plan to finish your schooling and job training."

We hugged in agreement. She was now ready to leave the nest and fly on her own.

Explore

✎ Describe how you could make (made) going on your own something you and your family could be (were) proud of. Be sure to consider the following areas in your plan.

Housing

_____

_____

_____

_____

Finances

_____

_____

_____

_____

Career Training

_____

_____

_____

_____

Friends and Acquaintances

_____

_____

_____

_____

The Discussions to Leave

_____

_____

_____

_____

Other

_____

_____

_____

_____

Thinking About This. When and how will you (did you) leave the nest? Will it be (was it) peaceably, with a plan or with torn feathers flying all over the place? (This question is confidential—so only share it with those you wish.)

Sharing (Family/Mate). How can a family be supportive of one who is taking off on their own? Role play the day of the leaving. How will you maintain contact? How will your relationship with that independent member change? What is dependence? What is independence? What is INTERdependence? What is INNERdependence?

Role play some other situations involving the "leaving" where the different types of dependence are displayed. Share your best role plays with the Community.

LEAVE HOME — REMAIN A FAMILY

> ***Challenge.*** *The Trobriand Indians of the South Pacific Islands kept their family ties throughout life. The young parents allowed the grandparents, aunts and uncles to use the wisdom of their years to help rear the children. The young parents then looked forward to later using their wisdom in rearing the children. But we have been taught that independence from family and others is a virtue. Some say this causes many families lose their sense of identity and fall apart. Perhaps we could learn from the Trobriands?*

Explore

✎ Describe three qualities your parent(s) have:

1. _____

_____

2. _____

_____

3. _____

_____

✎ How could you work it out so family and friends shared the privilege of rearing your children (not just "babysitting")?

_____

_____

_____

_____

✎ List three advantages to having others cooperate with you in your responsibilities.

1. _____

_____

2. _____

_____

3. _____

_____

✎ What three suggestions would you give someone who has a very "dysfunctional" family and doesn't like being with them?

1. _____

_____

2. _____

_____

3. _____

_____

✎ What change in attitude is necessary to remain a part of a family unit — yet be on your own. Be specific!

_____

_____

_____

_____

_____

_____

Thinking About This. How could a living situation be set up so there could be an extended family while also allowing for individual privacy and freedom?

Sharing (Family). Listen to each member's ideas and discuss the possibilities in your "real" family at home. Then, share your ideas with the Community.

HOUSE ON THE PRAIRIE

> **Challenge.** *Imagine for a few moments that you have entered the world of a hundred years ago. You are living in a little log cabin, nestled among the rolling hills.*

Explore

✎ What chores do you have today?

_____

_____

_____

_____

_____

✎ Who is around you and what are they doing?

_____

_____

_____

_____

_____

✎ What are you doing today that is enjoyable?

_____

_____

_____

_____

_____

✎ What challenges will you face today?

_____

_____

_____

_____

_____

✎ What are your greatest personal assets?

_____

_____

_____

_____

✎ How do these assets contribute to the community?

_____

_____

_____

_____

✎ How do you express your decision to be loving?

_____

_____

_____

_____

✎ How do you make the community part of your "extended" family?

_____

_____

_____

_____

Thinking About This. *What is the reality of my world today? How is it the same as 100 years ago? Different? How would I change my world? What must I accept that I cannot change? How do I do that? Who else is involved? Can I expect that person(s) to change? How? What are my dreams for my future?*

Sharing (Family/Mate/Friends). *As pioneers what major problems did you have to deal with? Pick one or two and role play—first to your Family and then with the Community.*

ACCEPTANCE

> **Challenge.** *"I like you—but, I am uncomfortable with some of the ways that you act."*

Explore

✎ Imagine that your town or city is a large box and each of you are animals running around in the box. Describe how your social life would change if the box was suddenly made much smaller.

_____

_____

_____

_____

_____

_____

✎ Write about feelings that you would have if each house was made of smaller squares and stacked 20 high on top of each other.

_____

_____

_____

_____

_____

✎ Now, imagine that the box representing your world is suddenly 100 times larger. How would your life be different?

_____

_____

_____

_____

_____

✎ How close do you want to live with others? Describe your distance (geographically and emotionally) to specific people in your life. (Don't place names or their roles — only your feelings and plans.)

Person #1: _____

_____

_____

_____

Person #2: _____

_____

_____

_____

Person #3: _____

_____

_____

_____

Thinking About This. *How close do I want to live to others? Is my need for space growing or shrinking? What am I doing about it? Are my feelings about privacy natural? When do I have too much space between me and others? What can I do about it? Who is responsibile for the degree of restriction or freedom that I now feel? Why? Does it change? How? Why?*

Sharing (Family). *Discuss specific ways to change your sense of restriction, sense of freedom. How can it be done with friendliness? With love and respect? Share examples of not-so-friendly conflict over space. What is "imposition?" "Territory?" "Boundries?" "Freedom?" "Relationships?" How is life like a dance? Describe your future "box."*

SIMULATION III — AND BABY MAKES THREE

An Extended Role Play for Mates and/or Families

Congratuations! You have a baby! Your instructor will decide at random if it is by birth, adoption or foster parent. Your VERY REAL task is to totally provide for the needs and wants of both the baby and yourselves as the parents. You will be fully responsible and accountable for the baby. You will make sure your baby's needs are FULLY MET 24-hours a day.

Your journal will reflect your total plan and how it was carried out. A babysitter cannot have the child more than eight hours a day. Again, you will enlist the help of the outside Community to learn of your baby's needs and meet them at least adaquately.

You WILL BE helped lovingly by your Mate, Friends, Family and the Leader in your responsibilities for the welfare of the child. (Remember, responsibility in planning and carrying out the plan is the only way to get the feeling of satisfaction!) The leader will assist you in setting the guidelines for the project.

✎ Have fun!

✎ Enjoyment!

✎ Satisfaction!

✎ Love!

✎ Growth!

✎ Plan It!

✎ Seek It!

✎ Keep it Light!

SELF-INVENTORY III

> **Challenge.** *This is another chance to evaluate myself. How am I doing so far? Before I begin answering these questions, I will review my responses in Section I and II and what I have learned about myself.*

Explore

✎ Ask yourself these questions honestly and with a fair degree of self-examination.

CHARACTERISTIC	CIRCLE ONE		
	LOW		HIGH
My Level of Sincerity			
Desire to do my best	1	2	3
Attempt to learn more	1	2	3
Wish to cooperate	1	2	3
My Research			
Use of many sources	1	2	3
Use of clear, straight-forward responses	1	2	3
Attempt to find more resources	1	2	3
My Awareness of Self			
Discovering new things	1	2	3
Desire to improve	1	2	3
Working on personal challenges	1	2	3
My Awareness of Others			
Level of ability to communicate ideas	1	2	3
Ability to assist others	1	2	3
My Written and Oral Products			
Quality of oral reports	1	2	3
Excellence of written work	1	2	3
Amount of preparation for work	1	2	3
The Carry-over Outside School			
Completed homework	1	2	3
Showed an acceptable degree of interest in my studies	1	2	3
Incorporated hobbies and interests that relate	1	2	3
Overall Sense of Personal Satisfaction			
Satisfaction in my personal growth	1	2	3
Ability to increase my friendships	1	2	3
Amount of available energy used	1	2	3
Degree I progressed toward my potential	1	2	3

FAMILY INVENTORY III

Challenge. *I will evaluate our Family honestly and lovingly.*

Explore

✎ Now that you have completed the Third Simulation in this book, express your opinions about your Family. Think carefully how your Family worked together.

CHARACTERISTIC	CIRCLE ONE		
	LOW		HIGH
Level Of Sincerity			
Our desire to do our best	1	2	3
Our attempt to learn more	1	2	3
Comments: _____			
Research			
Use of many sources	1	2	3
Clear, straight-forward sharing	1	2	3
Comments: _____			
Awareness			
Our attempt to listen to other's ideas	1	2	3
Effectiveness of Family communication	1	2	3
Comments: _____			
Cooperation			
Level at which we worked together	1	2	3
Our understanding of other's needs	1	2	3
Comments: _____			
Products			
Completion of our work	1	2	3
Clarity of our work	1	2	3
Appearance of our work	1	2	3
Comments: _____			

✎ I will use this format to make entries into our Journal to evaluate my Friends, Co-workers, and the Community.

SOME FINAL THOUGHTS

> ***Challenge.*** *Not one person in the world has the exact set of life challenges you have. YOU are uniquely qualified to handle the combinations life provides for you. YOU also are capable of creating life situations that fit YOU. YOUR attitude of I Can Manage Life will always work for YOU, moment-by-moment.*

Explore

✎ This guide to life experiences focused on four basic parts: "I," "CAN," "MANAGE," and "LIFE." You came into this program with knowledge and wisdom in each of these areas. Now, you have had a few months to experience more language of choice and growth.

✎ Use your Journal to take each word of the title of the program (I, CAN, MANAGE, LIFE) and write your thoughts about what you are discovering, learning, want to experience and desire to learn.

✎ Use your Journal to explore combinations of the words to express some unique thoughts you wish to share with your Family, Co-workers, Mates, Friends, and Community. Examples:

> • I CAN ...   • I ... LIFE   • CAN ... LIFE
> • I MANAGE   • ... MANAGE LIFE   • CAN ... MANAGE

> ***Putting It Together.*** *How has this program affected my life? What is its meaning to my past? Present? Future? How has my attitude changed toward schooling? Training? Co-workers, Family, Mate, Friends, Community? How can I continue this improvement in life? Choices? Growth? Why was the program subtitled Learning to Choose and Grow?*
>
> ***Sharing.*** *You decide how you wish to wrap-up and celebrate your experiences together. Show appreciation, warmth, caring, sharing—Love! The author (me) wishes to share my gratitude to you, my new friend! Thank you!*
> —*Loving,* **Dennis Hooker**

CONGRATULATIONS AND CERTIFICATE

Congratulations!

You have made many important decisions that brought you successfully to this point in your life. At times your life has "flowed" smoothly and with little effort. Sometimes you experienced conflicts, heartaches and discouragements.

You have weathered the storms and relaxed in the calms. You have thereby earned our official certificate granted to those who Manage Life.

This document gives you the permission to continue on your successful journey—moment-by-moment.

I CAN MANAGE LIFE

_____

Who has completed the program, "I Can Manage Life," earning the official certificate granted to those who MANAGE LIFE.

Signed _____
Author

Signed _____
Instructor / Facilitator

Date _____

More Good Books from JIST Works, Inc.

JIST publishes a variety of books on careers and job search topics. Please consider ordering one or more from your dealer, local bookstore, or directly from JIST.

Orders from Individuals: Please use the form below (or provide the same information) to order additional copies of this or other books listed on this page. You are also welcome to send us your order (please enclose money order, check, or credit card information), or simply call our toll free number at **1-800-648-JIST** or **1-317-264-3720**. Our FAX number is **1-317-264-3709**. **Qualified schools and organizations** may request our catalog and obtain information on quantity discounts (we have over 400 career-related books, videos, and other items).

Our offices are open weekdays 8 a.m. to 5 p.m. local time and our address is:

JIST Works, Inc. • 720 North Park Avenue • Indianapolis, IN 46202-3431

QTY	BOOK TITLE	TOTAL ($)
_____	*Getting the Job You Really Want*, J. Michael Farr •ISBN: 0-942784-15-4 • **$9.95**	_____
_____	*The Very Quick Job Search: Get a Good Job in Less Time*, J. Michael Farr •ISBN: 0-942784-72-3 • **$9.95**	_____
_____	*America's 50 Fastest Growing Jobs: An Authoritative Information Source* • ISBN: 0-942784-61-8 • **$10.95**	_____
_____	*America's Top 300 Jobs: A Complete Career Handbook* (trade version of the *Occupational Outlook Handbook* • ISBN 0-942784-45-6 • **$17.95**	_____
_____	*America's Federal Jobs: A Complete Directory of Federal Career Opportunities* • ISBN 0-942784-81-2 • **$14.95**	_____
_____	*The Resume Solution: How to Write and Use a Resume That Gets Results*, David Swanson • ISBN 0-942784-44-8 • **$10.95**	_____
_____	*The Job Doctor: Good Advice on Getting a Good Job*, Phillip Norris, Ed.D. • ISBN 0-942784-43-X • **$8.95**	_____
_____	*The Right Job for You: An Interactive Career Planning Guide*, J. Michael Farr • ISBN 0-942784-73-1 • **$9.95**	_____
_____	*Exploring Careers: A Young Person's Guide to over 300 Jobs* • ISBN 0-942784-27-8 • **$19.95**	_____
_____	*Work in the New Economy: Careers and Job Seeking into the 21st Century*, Robert Wegmann • ISBN 0-942784-19-78 • **$14.95**	_____
_____	*The Occupational Outlook Handbook* • ISBN 0-942784-38-3 • **$16.95**	_____
_____	*The Career Connection: Guide to College Majors and Their Related Careers*, Dr. Fred Rowe • ISBN 0-942784-82-0 • **$15.95**	_____
_____	*The Career Connection II: Guide to Technical Majors and Their Related Careers*, Dr. Fred Rowe • ISBN 0-942784-83-9 • **$13.95**	_____
_____	*Career Emphasis: Making Good Decisions* • ISBN 0-942784-10-3 • **$6.95**	_____
_____	*Career Emphasis: Preparing for Work* • ISBN 0-942784-11-1 • **$6.95**	_____
_____	*Career Emphasis: Getting a Good Job and Getting Ahead* • ISBN 0-942784-13-8 • **$6.95**	_____
_____	*Career Emphasis: Understanding Yourself* • ISBN 0-942784-12-X • **$6.95**	_____
_____	*Career & Life Skills: Making Decisions* • ISBN 0-942784-57-X • **$6.95**	_____
_____	*Career & Life Skills: Knowing Yourself* • ISBN 0-942784-58-8 • **$6.95**	_____
_____	*Career & Life Skills: Your Career* • ISBN 0-942784-60-X • **$6.95**	_____
_____	*Career & Life Skills: Career Preparation* • ISBN 0-942784-59-6 • **$6.95**	_____
_____	*Living Skills Series: Effective Communication Skills* • ISBN 1-56370-038-7 942784-57-X • **$7.95**	_____
_____	*Living Skills Series Why Should I Hire You?* • ISBN 1-56730-039-5 • **$6.95**	_____
_____	*Living Skills Series: The Two Best Ways to Find A Job* • ISBN 1-56370-040-9 • **$6.95**	_____
_____	*I Am (Already) Successful*, Dennis Hooker • ISBN 0-942784-41-3 • **$6.95**	_____
_____	*I Can Manage Life*, Dennis Hooker • ISBN 0-942784-77-4 • **$8.95**	_____
_____	*Young Person's Guide to Getting and Keeping a Good Job*, J. Michael Farr & Marie Pavlicko • ISBN 0-942784-34-0 • **$6.95**	_____
_____	*Job Savvy*, LaVerne Ludden• ISBN 0-942784-79-0 • **$10.95**	_____

Subtotal _____

Sales Tax _____

Shipping: ($3 for first book, $1 for each additional book.) _____

(Prices subject to change without notice) (U.S. Currency only) TOTAL ENCLOSED WITH ORDER _____

❑ Check ❑ Money order   Credit Card: ❑ MasterCard ❑ VISA ❑ AMEX

Card # (if applies)_____Exp. Date_____

Name (please print) _____

Name of Organization (if applies) _____

Address_____

City/State/Zip_____

Daytime Telephone (   ) _____ — _____

Thank-you for your order!